1000 All New Millie Bobby Brown Facts

Mera Wolfe

Contents

INTRODUCTION

1000 All New Millie Bobby Brown Facts contains a further ALL NEW 1000 facts about this acting superstar. Facts about Stranger Things 4, Enola Holmes 2, fashion, food, lifestyle, homes, celebrity friends, Kong vs Godzilla, Damsel, Jake Bongiovi, Florence By Mills, pets, likes and dislikes, The Electric State and so much more all awaits in 1000 All New Millie Bobby Brown Facts.

1000 ALL NEW MILLIE BOBBY BROWN FACTS

(1) Millie often does the 'floss dance' to amuse herself between takes on a set. This dance is often assumed to have originated from the game Fortnite but was apparently invented by 'Instagram star' Russell Horning, aka The Backpack Kid.

(2) Although some people seem to assume that all the youngsters in Stranger Things are preposterously older than the characters they play, Millie was only 17 years-old when she began shooting Stranger Things 4. It's not as if she was a 35 year-old pretending to be a high schooler!

(3) According to industry experts, Millie was the third highest paid female actor in the world in 2022. Only Margot Robbie and Lady Gaga earned more money for acting.

(4) Eleven had her short buzzcut hair from season one again in Stranger Things 4 but Millie didn't have to shave her head this time. What they did instead was simply slick back Millie's hair and stuff it under a short haired wig. It was convincing enough in the end. This was no mean feat because her hair was shoulder length at the time. The makeup department had to study Millie's head shape and hairline to make the short haired wig as realistic looking as possible.

(5) After working with Millie again on Stranger Things 4, Matthew Modine said she reminded him of a young Natalie Wood. Natalie Wood was a famous dark-haired Oscar nominated actress who began acting at the age of four and

later appeared in classic films like Rebel without a Cause,
The Searchers, and West Side Story.

(6) Millie's salary on Enola Holmes 2 was the largest ever
paid to an actor under the age of 20.

(7) Millie says that when she orders drive-thru food in
America she still occasionally has incidents where they
don't understand her accent!

(8) Millie said she loves the smell of pumpkins.

(9) Millie uses a Peloton exercise bike to keep fit. She said
she usually listens to Taylor Swift when she does this.

(10) Enola Holmes 2 uses the Matchgirls' Strike of 1888 as
part of its plot. This was a real event where young girls who
worked by dipping poplar sticks into white phosphorus to
make matchsticks protested at their poor and dangerous
working conditions. The Matchgirls' Strike of 1888 was led
by female workers at the Bryant and May match factory in
London. The strike began on July 2, 1888, and lasted for two
weeks, resulting in improved working conditions and better
pay for the matchgirls.

(11) Finn Wolfhard said that when he had to kiss Millie in
the season one finale of Stranger Things he sort of
accidentally head-butted her. This must be why Millie
famously didn't seem to enjoy the kiss very much at the
time!

(12) Millie said she has taken to mixing a personal 'cocktail'
of different fragrances so that she has her own unique smell
and isn't wearing the same fragrance as anyone else.

(13) Millie says that her deafness in one ear is not curable and something she has learned to live with.

(14) Millie's overnight fame through Stranger Things was probably magnified by the fact that she was the lone girl among the kids in season one. This and the fact that her character was very cultish and memorable made her more unique than the boys and the magazines and media tended to gravitate towards her somewhat more than Finn, Gaten, Caleb, or Noah. The fact that she 'shared' this exposure and sudden fame with four other kids was definitely a help though and they were very much a gang in their early media interviews.

(15) Millie said that when she makes gravy she always adds some Marmite to give it more flavour. Marmite is a yeast spread that people either seem to love or hate.

(16) Millie did a Q&A in 2018 which revealed that she'd never heard of K-Pop and had no idea who BTS were.

(17) Though she was born in Marbella, Millie says she doesn't really have any childhood memories of Spain because she only lived there for the first three or four years of her life.

(18) Millie said she met her boyfriend Jake Bongiovi on Instagram.

(19) The body double for the young 1979 lab version of Eleven in Stranger Things 4 was child actor Martie Blair. Blair was best known for playing Bella in the soap opera The Young and the Restless. CGI was used to impose the likeness of a younger Millie over Blair's face. Although Martie Blair resembles a nine year-old version of Millie they

decided this would be the most realistic thing to do. Martie Blair worked a lot with Millie on the set in order to mimic Millie's body language and movements as Eleven. The results were certainly impressive - aside from one slightly awkward shot where the young Eleven is looking up at Henry Creel. During post-production Millie had to use something called the Lola machine to copy Martie's movements so that her likeness could be imposed.

(20) In an interview with Allure, Millie once expressed an eccentric dislike of men who carry umbrellas!

(21) The futuristic bathing costume that Millie as Eleven wears in the lab scenes in season one of Stranger Things and Stranger Things 4 is a haptic suit. Haptic technology is technology that can create an experience of touch by applying forces, vibrations, or motions to the user. The suit in season one was beige and had rectangle blocks which acted as weights so that Eleven could sink into the sensory deprivation water tank. In season four the suit was white to make it more stark in the underground lab and the rectangle blocks on the suit were actually floats this time so that Eleven could float in the water tank. The concept behind the suit is that this is essentially Eleven's superhero costume.

(22) In 2023, it was reported that Millie visited London's Metal Morphosis piercing studio and asked for lobe, helix and navel piercings. She was warned that having all these piercings done in one day might hurt but staff said Millie 'took it like a champ' and didn't flinch once.

(23) The 1979 version of Eleven makes a 'superhero landing' (head down, on one knee, arms apart) in the Stranger Things episode The Massacre at Hawkins Lab after

vanquishing Henry Creel at the lab - which cross-cuts with Eleven's powers returning in 1986 as she floats in the sensory deprivation water chamber. This is a nice payoff given Eleven's depression earlier in the season at the loss of her powers. She's a superhero once again. The 'superhero landing' (mocked in Deadpool) is associated with characters like Black Widow in the Marvel movies but goes way back. Iron Man has been depicted with his own unique 'landing' in the comics for decades. You can see examples of the superhero landing in Japanese anime, The Matrix trilogy, and the Blade movies with Wesley Snipes - which all obviously predate the MCU.

(24) Millie says that chamomile tea helps her to sleep.

(25) Millie is right-handed.

(26) Millie said she quite likes Huevos rancheros for breakfast or lunch. This consists of fried eggs served on lightly fried or charred corn or flour tortillas topped with a pico de gallo made of tomatoes, chili peppers, onion, and cilantro.

(27) In order to get the likeness for the 1979 version of Eleven in Stranger Things 4 the special effects department used clips from Once Upon a Time in Wonderland - which Millie appeared in when she was nine years-old - as a reference.

(28) According to Millie she now has seven tattoos. They seem to be very small tattoos where you wouldn't even notice them at first glance.

(29) A baseball painted by the artist Charles Fazzino and signed by Millie fetched around $2,000 on a memorabilia

site.

(30) Millie said that her favourite toy as a child was a toy microphone which enabled her to sing along to High School Musical songs.

(31) Millie and Jake Bongiovi visited a bee farm in 2022 and did some beekeeping for the day.

(32) Millie starred in the 2021 sequel Godzilla vs. Kong. This was one of those films affected by the pandemic - as a consequence of which its release date kept being pushed back and it had to rely on streaming in addition to a theatrical release in order to have any hope of recouping its large production budget. The film earned pretty good reviews and although it wasn't a blockbuster it did well enough not to lose money.

(33) Millie said she watched a lot of Wizards Of Waverly Place when she was a kid. This was a Disney sitcom show which launched Selena Gomez on the path to fame.

(34) Millie has a donkey called Bernard. She gave this donkey a mention in a social media post on her 18th birthday.

(35) Millie says she loves parsnips - especially with a roast dinner. Parsnips are a very sweet vegetable and what you might describe as an acquired taste.

(36) In Stranger Things 4, Eleven has to go into a sensory deprivation tank in the missile silo in order to retrieve her memories and get her powers back. Millie said she had a couple of days where she spent up to ten hours a day in the tank and suffered from claustrophobia as a

consequence. The water had salt so she could float and they
had to use a microphone to relay instructions because it
was difficult for her to hear anything due to the fact that her
ears were often underwater!

(37) The famous racing driver Lewis Hamilton once took
Millie for a spin in a Mercedes-AMG GT R when she visited a
racetrack.

(38) The Conan Doyle estate sued Netflix over the first
Enola Holmes movie for its depiction of a kinder and more
human Sherlock Holmes. They argued that this facet of the
character only appeared in later Sherlock Holmes books
that are still copywrited. Sherlock Holmes is rather strange
when it comes to iconic characters in that he is public
domain and so literally anyone can make a Sherlock Holmes
movie. This is very different to James Bond - the film rights
to which are owned by the Broccoli family company EON
and MGM/Amazon. If you tried to make an unofficial Bond
film you'd be sued and taken to court so quickly your feet
wouldn't touch the ground.

(39) Millie has joked that the last ever episode of Stranger
Things should be a musical special with the characters all
constantly breaking into song.

(40) Millie said she used to use hairspray to 'tame' her
eyebrows.

(41) The Electric State movie, in which Millie is the lead, is
based on an illustrated novel by Simon Stålenhag. The
synopsis for the book is - "In 1997, a runaway teenager and
her yellow toy robot travel west through a strange USA. The
ruins of gigantic battle drones litter the countryside, heaped
together with the discarded trash of a high tech

consumerist society in decline. As their car approaches the edge of the continent, the world outside the window seems to be unraveling ever faster—as if somewhere beyond the horizon, the hollow core of civilization has finally caved in."

(42) The Electric State is directed by the Russo Brothers - who are best known for directing the last two Avengers films in the Marvel universe.

(43) Millie has a pet rabbit called Eeyore. She said she sometimes sneaks this rabbit into hotels.

(44) The reason why Millie couldn't shave her hair off again for Stranger Things 4 is not because she wasn't willing but because she had too many other contracted professional commitments at the time which made this impossible.

(45) Millie said she would be up for playing Britney Spears in a biopic.

(46) Millie is a big fan of Yorkshire pudding. Yorkshire puddings are a British tradition with roast dinners.

(47) Millie said she now plays a few video games and enjoys Sims 4 and Fortnite.

(48) Millie isn't part of the cast for Godzilla vs. Kong 2. It appears that with The Electric State and her ongoing commitments to Stranger Things taking up her time she decided to duck out of giant fighting monster capers for the time being.

(49) Millie and Noah Schnapp have joked that they have a 'marriage pact' where they will marry each other if they are both single at the age of 40. They do stress though that their

relationship and close bond is strictly platonic.

(50) Charlotte and Clara Ward are the twins who played the baby Eleven in the Stranger Things 2 flashbacks set in the lab of Dr Brenner. Like the Price twins (who portray Holly Wheeler in Stranger Things), Charlotte and Clara have also portrayed Judith Grimes in The Walking Dead. So if you add Martie Blair and Millie, four people have now portrayed Eleven in Stranger Things.

(51) It is estimated that Eleven kills (appropriately enough) eleven people in the first season of Stranger Things. Her victims are all lab workers or government agents.

(52) Enola Holmes uses a bit of jiu-jitsu in her fights. Jiu-jitsu is a martial art in which you use holds, throws, and 'grappling' to defeat your foe.

(53) In the Enola Holmes movies, Millie's character often breaks the 'fourth wall' and talks directly to the camera. Millie said this was inspired by Phoebe Waller-Bridge in the comedy show Fleabag. Millie said that she would do this in virtually every scene and then they would just use the funniest ones and cut out the 'fourth wall' moments which didn't work so well. It is obviously no coincidence that Fleabag and Enola Holmes have the same director.

(54) Millie has stayed at the SonevaFushi resort in the Maldives. Prices for this resort apparently start at about $2,000 a night!

(55) Millie attended the BRIT Awards in 2018. She presented an award with Kylie Minogue.

(56) In 2020, Millie appeared in Mariah Carey's Magical

Christmas Special as herself.

(57) The missile silo where Eleven regains her powers in Stranger Things 4 was designed to look like a real Cold War missile silo. The production designers used declassified military documents to create the look of the set. The set was 300 foot long and deliberately designed to be claustrophobic.

(58) Millie's collaboration with EA Games on the video game The Sims 4 was themed around a positivity challenge where characters were encouraged to perform kind tasks.

(59) In 2022, Millie enrolled as an online student at Purdue University studying the 'human services program'. Purdue University is a public land-grant research university in West Lafayette, Indiana. Millie couldn't go to university in the traditional way because she was too busy with her acting career.

(60) Millie is apparently quite fond of coffee ice cream.

(61) Millie has now attended over 40 comic cons.

(62) Millie said she is able to cry on cue for a scene - should tears be required.

(63) Millie says she does most on her online college work in her trailer while she's waiting to be called back to the set for a scene.

(64) Millie has been spotted dining at Sheesh Chigwell - which is a restaurant in Essex. The eatery is in Ye Olde Kings Head in Chigwell, an inn that dates back to 1547. This restaurant is known for its Turkish food and seems to

attract a lot of reality TV stars. Celebrities like Tyson Fury, Harry Kane, and Harry Styles have also been seen dining here.

(65) When she shot the scenes in Stranger Things 4 of Eleven in the roller rink, Millie took some spins around the rink in her skates between takes purely for fun. Roller rinks were very big in the 1980s but they aren't nearly as common today.

(66) Millie's buzzcut wig in season Stranger Things 4 had to withstand desert sandstorms and a water tank. It's incredible really that it managed to survive all of this!

(67) In May 2022, Millie became a house ambassador for Louis Vuitton.

(68) Millie said she often sings along to Harry Styles songs when she's driving.

(69) Millie said she was rooting for Godzilla in Godzilla vs. Kong because she had previously appeared in a Godzilla movie and so felt a sense of loyalty to him!

(70) Jamie Campbell Bower said that Millie was a bit tearful and overwhelmed at first when she had to do close up scenes with him in his frightening Vecna make-up in Stranger Things 4. He had to remind Millie that it was simply him in a suit and not a real monster!

(71) Some fans of Stranger Things found it rather disappointing that in season four the character of Eleven has been adopted by Joyce Byers and yet Millie and Winona Ryder barely say a word to each other in the entire season! It would have been nice to see these two actors share at

least a couple of proper scenes.

(72) Eleven's main foe in Stranger Things 4 is named Vecna by the kids. Vecna was a wizard in Dungeons & Dragons. The character is known as the God of Secrets. Vecna was first referenced in OD&D's third supplement, Eldritch Wizardry.

(73) Millie said that when she started acting her parents encouraged her to watch old films made long before she was born. She said she was inspired by all the great actors she discovered this way.

(74) Millie says she is a big fan of the HBO show The White Lotus.

(75) Millie has said that she thinks Enola Holmes is more of a superhero than Eleven because she doesn't have any superpowers and has to rely on her wits and fortitude.

(76) Millie said she snacks on fruit a lot when she's working.

(77) When Eleven learns the terrible origin of Vecna/Henry Creel in The Massacre at Hawkins Lab, the music playing is by award winning composer Philip Glass from the film Koyaanisqatsi. Koyaanisqatsi is a cult 1982 film directed by Godfrey Reggio with cinematography by Ron Fricke. The film is a visual documentary featuring time lapse photography.

(78) Millie says she turns off all of her gadgets late at night so she can relax.

(79) Social media posts show Millie's bedroom in Atlanta

has grey and white furnishings and that she seems to be fond of lamps.

(80) Millie said that when she went to primary school in England she used to sing Rihanna songs in the morning to wake herself up.

(81) Millie has a habit of taking her shoes off for magazine interviews. She said she much prefers being barefoot to wearing shoes.

(82) Millie uses tea tree oil spot stickers to deal with skin blemishes.

(83) Millie said one of the reasons why she wanted to do Enola Holmes is that there didn't seem to be many British female heroes as the lead in films. Famous British hero characters like Sherlock Holmes, Harry Potter, Robin Hood, and James Bond are all male.

(84) Millie often does makeup sessions on Instagram where she begins barefaced with some blemishes and red spots. She thinks it is important for people to see that celebrities are human and don't have perfect crystal glass skin. When you see celebrities in magazines they have had a professional makeup session and also been digitally airbrushed. No one actually looks like that in real life.

(85) Eleven doesn't seem to kill anyone in Stranger Things 2 - which is a rare occurrence in the show.

(86) Before the 2014 show Intruders (in which Millie had an early role) came out, Millie's Intruders co-star John Simm told the media that she would be a superstar one day.

(87) On her press junket for Enola Holmes 2, Millie was asked once and for all if she liked eggo waffles and gave a firm no. She doesn't like eggo waffles and uses a spit bucket if she has to eat them in Stranger Things. Millie enjoys carrots, cheese, avocados, salads, and various foods but eggo waffles will not be found in her grocery basket.

(88) The popular BBC television show Sherlock with Benedict Cumberbatch introduced a sister to Sherlock and Mycroft named Eurus Holmes. However, the Enola Holmes books predated this so you could say this idea had already been done (though Eurus, unlike Enola, was a villain).

(89) Asked who she thought the best ever Sherlock Holmes was, Millie replied by saying Henry Cavill. Millie could hardly say anything else could she? There have been many fantastic performances by actors playing the great detective - in particular Basil Rathbone, Jeremy Brett, Peter Cushing, Robert Stephens, Douglas Wilmar, and Benedict Cumberbatch.

(90) Notice that Eleven has a scar on her shin in the roller rink in Stranger Things 4. This is from where the Flayer parasite was removed in season three.

(91) Millie celebrated her nineteenth birthday by going clubbing in Los Angeles.

(92) The father of Millie's boyfriend is John Francis Bongiovi Jr - better known by his professional name Jon Bon Jovi. Jon Bon Jovi is best known as the founder and frontman of the rock band Bon Jovi.

(93) Millie once turned up to an interview for Allure at Wentworth golf club in pj's and a cardigan. This is what you

could call dressing down!

(94) If you were wondering why Millie was interviewed at a golf course it was because it was near a house she'd moved into. She doesn't actually play golf herself. Wentworth Club is a privately owned golf club and country club in Virginia Water, Surrey, on the south western fringes of London, not far from Windsor Castle.

(95) Millie says she channels some of her own awkwardness into the character of Eleven.

(96) Millie says she has her own office in her house. She said she finds it relaxing to just sit in there alone for a bit of peace and quiet.

(97) The steam train in the first Enola Holmes movie is a GWR 28XX freight loco.

(98) Eleven has a poster for the film For the Love of Benji in her bedroom in Stranger Things 4. This is the second in a series of family films about the adventures of a golden mixed breed dog named Benji.

(99) Millie has been seen dining at Sketch Restaurant in London. This is a swanky restaurant with striking decor. Afternoon tea for one there will set you back £60.

(100) There have been a number of Stranger Things comics. One that is quite Eleven-centric is titled Stranger Things: Winter Special. This takes place after the events of season two and has Hopper sneaking Eleven out to the Byers house for Christmas. This comic is largely plotless and descends into the characters telling various Christmas stories. While the comic is quite sweet (in that the traditions of Christmas

and gifts are all new to Eleven) it is also very inconsequential and aimless and doesn't really linger in the memory much afterwards. This comic is an example of how Stranger Things comics are frequently hobbled by the stipulation not to tread on the grass trodden by the television show. As a consequence you tend to get these little side stories set between seasons. While it is pleasant to spend more time with these characters the actual stories are rarely that eventful or interesting. Stranger Things: Winter Special is a case in point.

(101) Millie's somewhat curly hair in Stranger Things 3 is not a perm. That's her natural hair.

(102) Millie says she has written two screenplays with her sister Paige. One of the scripts is about their grandmother.

(103) When Eleven confronts Henry Creel at the lab in The Massacre at Hawkins Lab the rainbow pattern on the wall behind Henry is upside down. This is a nice piece of visual foreshadowing.

(104) Millie said that when she has a roast dinner she always has peas, carrots, asparagus, green beans, and turnips as the vegetables.

(105) When she drives a car with the top down, Millie often wears a back to front cap to keep her hair out of her eyes.

(106) Millie said that making films like Godzilla vs. Kong is a strange experience because you have to do a lot of reactions to nothing on the set and it is only months later when the monsters and backdrops have been put in through digital special effects that you actually see what the film looks like.

(107) When she used to sing songs on her old (long defunct) YouTube channel, Millie simply called herself Millie Brown. The 'Bobby' was only added later.

(108) Enola Holmes 2 spent four weeks in Netflix's Top 10 most streamed shows and movies.

(109) Millie is a fan of the black comedy film Jojo Rabbit.

(110) The main inspiration for Vecna in Stranger Things 4 was Pinhead in the Hellraiser horror franchise. Though grotesque and wicked, Pinhead was a rather urbane and chatty sort of horror monster. You could say the same of Vecna.

(111) Millie said that when she first became a child actor she had no idea what she was doing. It was only through experience that she got better.

(112) Millie is a big fan of Greek salad. As you probably know, this consists of tomatoes, cucumbers, onion, feta cheese, and olives.

(113) In the Eleven-centric Stranger Things 4 episode The Nina Project, Dr Brenner references 'Nina, ou La folle par amour' (Nina, or The Woman Crazed with Love) - an opéra-comique in one act by the French composer Nicolas Dalayrac. This music was used in one of the season four teaser trailers. The plot of this opera has a woman named Nina suffering from a diagnosis of psychogenic amnesia after she is led to believe that her lover has been killed in a duel. Nina loses all sense of reason in her troubled state.

(114) Millie said that she's a bit of a contradiction in that she's a tomboy but also gets excited by pink things and

roses.

(115) Millie had to go to Australia to shoot Godzilla vs. Kong. Warner Bros have a substantial studio facility there and use it for many of their films. The film also shot some scenes in Hawaii.

(116) David Harbour (who plays Hopper) said that he does sometimes worry some of the younger cast members in Stranger Things like Millie might never quite know what it is like to have a normal life because they all became famous while they were still children. David said he was quite thankful that he only became famous in his forties. He doesn't think he could have coped with fame when he was a teenager.

(117) Ross Duffer, who created Stranger Things with his brother Matt, said that Winona Ryder, who was famous herself at a tender age, has been helpful in talking to Millie about the pressures of fame and celebrity. "She's talked to the kids about what celebrity is like and how the press can be and the anxiety and confusion that comes along with celebrity. I think she's really helped them. I know she's specifically helped Millie a lot to work through that. And that's something that no one else can help with, really, because so few people have experienced it. It's not something I understand. It's not something that, you know, even a parent would understand."

(118) Millie directed a short commercial for Samsung on her phone. You could say that this was her directorial debut. She also narrated the commercial.

(119) When she first became famous, Millie was rather bemused and baffled by the amount of American

interviewers who thought she was Australian.

(120) A magazine who interviewed Millie said that her dad
fetched her a cup of tea and some chocolate biscuits during
the interview. Tea is obviously an essential for Millie.

(121) Millie says her favourite number is 8 specifically
because this is the number that Steven Gerrard wore when
he played football for Liverpool. Gerrard made over 500
appearances for Liverpool and also captained England.

(122) In the first Enola Holmes movie, Enola and her
mother seem to be fond of beekeeping. This is the pastime
that Sherlock Holmes takes up in the Conan-Doyle books
when he retires.

(123) Eleven kills an estimated two people in Stranger
Things 4 - the pilot and gunner of the helicopter trying to
kill her in Papa. One could add Henry Creel too if we count
the 1979 flashbacks. Eleven is sometimes assumed to have
killed three orderlies when her powers briefly return in The
Nina Project. One assumes though that they could have
survived - albeit with plenty of bruises for their trouble!

(124) Millie thinks she nailed her Stranger Things audition
because she went into it feeling as if she had nothing to lose.

(125) Competitive eating champion Joey Chestnut set a
record in 2019 when he ate 81 frozen Eggo waffles in eight
minutes. Millie would shudder at the mere thought!

(126) One of Millie's tattoos is a small heart.

(127) Millie says that she prefers to have short hair in real
life because it is less hassle and easier to manage. As she

points out, you can always wear extensions or a wig if you want to go 'glam' for a night out.

(128) Millie secured financial backing from Legendary Pictures for the Enola Holmes movie while she was appearing in Godzilla: King of the Monsters for them.

(129) The short wig that Millie wears in Stranger Things 4 was a long wig cut down by the hairdressing department. Due to child labour laws, the hairdressing department had to learn how to apply the wig to Millie in no more than 35 minutes.

(130) Millie went into partnership with Essentia Water in 2023.

(131) Millie is a big fan of the animated film The Incredibles.

(132) Millie seems to have a few neon lights in her bedroom if her social media posts are anything to go by.

(133) Enola Holmes 2 shot some scenes at Chatham Dockyard in Kent. This was once a historic Royal Navy dockyard but is now a visitor attraction and museum.

(134) Millie said that one of her duties on Enola Holmes 2 as a producer was to watch the dailies. This is the raw unedited footage shot each day. Dailies are constantly reviewed and watched because the production needs to make sure that each scene had enough camera coverage and did not suffer from any technical problems (like a smudgy lens). Dailies are also useful in reviewing the performances of the actors and deciding if they need to change anything in the way they are playing their part.

(135) The Stranger Things writers named Welcome to the Dollhouse as one of the films they discussed when planning Eleven's early scenes in season four. Welcome to the Dollhouse is a 1995 American coming-of-age black comedy by Todd Solondz and stars Heather Matarazzo (no relation to Gaten despite the surname) as a shy seventh-grader who is hopelessly adrift trying to fit in with kids her own age at school.

(136) Millie says she begins each day by drinking half a bottle of water.

(137) Among the magazines Millie has now appeared on the cover of are In Style, Elle, Deadline, Bazaar, Glamour, Vogue, Teenvogue, Marie Claire, Vanity Fair, Miss, SFX, Supercoool, and T magazine.

(138) Millie's autograph in and of itself isn't worth that much but if you have a good piece of merch (like an 8-bit Eleven Funko) signed by Millie then you could be sitting on a nice little earner and make yourself upwards of $350.

(139) Millie said she can't help binging Love Island on television.

(140) Millie likes to roast potatoes in rosemary and canola oil.

(141) On her 18th birthday, Millie went to the Cirque Le Soir nightclub and the Windmill club in London with her boyfriend Jake Bongiovi. Millie wore a draped slip dress accentuated by the woven corset crafted from a mixed vintage French tapestry. She also seemed to be sporting a Barbie like blonde wig.

(142) In the original plan for Stranger Things 2, Eleven was going to 'mercy kill' her catatonic mother Teresa 'Terry' Ives. Upon reflection though the writers decided this might be rather too dark and so excised this detail from the scripts.

(143) Millie says she always has a bottle of water in her bag so she can stay hydrated.

(144) Stranger Things 4 is the first season of the show where we see Eleven attending a school.

(145) Millie has posted a picture on Instagram of herself and Jake Bongiovi enjoying the London Eye. The London Eye is basically a giant ferris wheel on the South Bank of the River Thames. It is Europe's tallest cantilevered observation wheel and a hugely popular attraction.

(146) Millie said that when they wrapped shooting on Stranger Things 4 she and some of the crew pranked Noah Schnapp by springing an ambush on him involving water balloons.

(147) Millie said that she was once pulled over by a police officer while driving in America but he recognised her from Stranger Things so she didn't get a ticket. You could call this one of the perks of fame!

(149) Enola Holmes filmed some scenes in Dorchester Prison in Dorset. This was a real prison which closed in 2013.

(150) Millie went straight from shooting Stranger Things 4 in the New Mexico desert to shooting Enola Holmes 2 in the middle of a British winter. The plunge in temperature must

have been quite a shock to the system one would imagine.

(151) Millie was seen dining at the Hollywood restaurant Tao in 2018. This is a Chinese restaurant which is part of the Tao chain. The Hollywood Tao apparently seems to attract a lot of celebrities although some of the critic reviews have been a trifle snooty about the food there.

(152) Millie says it was just a coincidence that she enrolled in an online college course at an Indiana (where Millie has a home and Stranger Things is shot) university. Given that she's an online student she presumably could have chosen anywhere.

(153) Millie said she watched the classic Mafia crime drama film The Godfather when she only eight years-old. The Godfather is probably not a film that eight year-olds should really be watching because it has some very violent moments.

(154) There were rumours a few years ago that Millie was in talks to play Batgirl in a DC Comics movie. Maybe it's just as well these rumours were false because they did actually make a Batgirl movie but decided not to release it because it was deemed 'unreleasable'. Some industry observers think they did this as a tax-write off but it could simply be the case that the film really was that bad.

(155) Millie said she doesn't like foaming cleansers because they can be a bit messy.

(156) One of Millie's tattoos is a 011 in tribute to her character in Stranger Things.

(157) Millie said people should always remember that

famous people are not perfect and only human.

(158) Millie said she tends to do her makeup on the production set rather than at home in the morning.

(159) Millie is a big fan of Kristin Ess shampoo and conditioner.

(160) Millie enjoys embroidery as a hobby.

(161) Millie earned $10 million for appearing in Enola Holmes 2.

(162) Millie said she put a lot of thought in the accent for Enola Holmes. She didn't want Enola to sound posh or like a cockney Victorian street urchin so she had to find a logical middle ground.

(163) Millie's other rabbit is called Bellatrix.

(164) Millie and Jake Bongiovi first came out as a couple on the BAFTA red carpet.

(165) Millie spent a lot of early 2023 with long blonde hair. This is because that is her character's look in The Electric State film she was shooting.

(166) For the death scene of (spoiler alert) Brenner when he's with Eleven in Stranger Things 4, the Duffer Brothers said that Millie rather amazingly nailed this emotional scene perfectly in only two takes.

(167) Millie made a 'generous' donation in 2023 to the Earthquake appeal seeking to help those affected in Turkey and Syria.

(168) Millie said that when she worked on the Enola Holmes movies she quickly learned that Henry Cavill doesn't talk about his private life. He likes to keep that completely, well, private! She said that Henry is very nice and they are good friends on the set but he's just a very private person.

(169) The Netflix streaming service overloaded and crashed for about half an hour when Volume 2 of Stranger Things 4 was dropped on the site.

(170) A number of scenes for Enola Holmes 2 were shot in the city of Hull. The red brick buildings in the old town area were deemed perfect for a Victorian atmosphere.

(171) Millie says that getting a bit older means the parts she can play are becoming more flexible. She's obviously out of that stage now where she plays little kids.

(172) The director on Enola Holmes 2 said the cameras had a difficult time keeping up with Millie because she's full of energy and always moving a lot during scenes.

(173) Millie got to know Mariah Carey because Mariah said that her son was a big Stranger Things fan and wanted to meet Millie.

(174) Millie says that Matthew Modine is the tidiest cast member on Stranger Things. There is never clutter in his dressing room and he always has fresh flowers on his desk.

(175) At the time of writing, Millie has a shade over 63 million followers on Instagram.

(176) What with Stranger Things and Enola Holmes, Millie

says she is becoming a dab hand at performing stunts now. They obviously don't let actors do anything TOO dangerous though.

(177) Eleven's clothes at the start of Stranger Things 4 are deliberately mismatched to reflect her confused state of mind. Without her powers and bereft of Hopper and Hawkins, Eleven doesn't really know who she is anymore.

(178) There was a lot of speculation that Millie was going to be in the Marvel film The Eternals but this turned out to have no basis in fact. Millie said she was baffled by the speculation because she'd never had any contact with Marvel.

(179) The arrival of 2023 meant that Millie had now been an actor for a whole decade (her first credits were in 2013). One could say then that Millie is what you might describe as a young veteran.

(180) Millie said she wouldn't want to be asked to direct a film just because she's a famous actor. She'd rather feel like she'd earned an opportunity like that through hard work and experience.

(181) Eleven kills four people in Stranger Things 3. These were Russian baddies at the mall. Eleven threw a car at them with her mind powers to save her friends!

(182) Millie was delighted that Eleven was adopted by Joyce Byers at the end of Stranger Things 3 because it meant she finally got some scenes with Noah Schnapp. Millie and Noah are best friends in real life but their characters barely say a word to each other in the first three seasons of the show. While the characters of Eleven and

Will Byers are not exactly chatterboxes and don't have long endless conversations in season four at the very least we do actually see them together for a change.

(183) Female empowerment coach and author Gifty Enright said of Millie - "She has that special blend of glamour, talent and substance. Brands want to be about substance and be seen to care about real issues and she presents them with that opportunity. The fate of people who become stars at a young age is that they risk being frozen into the frame of their youth and they are not allowed to break out of that by growing up, which is unrealistic. Also being a woman means Millie has to walk a sort of tightrope – of growing up as a woman in the public eye and staying relatable and not be judged by her looks alone. Luckily for her, she came into the public eye for her talent and for the causes she championed. Those things are not transient. As long as she keeps them at the centre of what she does, then she will be fine."

(184) Mike Wheeler isn't too convinced by pineapple on pizza in Stranger Things 4 but Eleven seems to like it. The first person to put pineapple on pizza was said to be Sam Panopoulos. He was a Greek immigrant who moved to Canada in 1954 and created the first Hawaiian pizza at his restaurant.

(185) It would probably be fair to say that the huge success of Stranger Things took the cast and crew by surprise. Most of them didn't even expect to get a second season.

(186) The reason why Mycroft Holmes doesn't return in Enola Holmes 2 is that the actor Sam Clafin had a scheduling conflict. He was working on another film and wasn't available. Clafin said he would like to return though if future Enola Holmes films are made.

(187) Lt. Colonel Sullivan reveals in Stranger Things 4 that Eleven was apparently being trained by Brenner to be an assassin by means of remote viewing. If that is the case one can see why they were so desperate to recapture her in season one.

(188) The house in California where Eleven lives with the Byers family in Stranger Things 4 was found by the production crew in Albuquerque's Glenwood Hills community. They had originally planned to construct a house themselves but found exactly what they were looking for as this real house had Poltergeist/E.T Spielberg vibes and also outdated fittings and fixtures which made it already feel like a period home even before anything was done. About a month after season four wrapped, the house was put on the market and became an Airbnb starting at $400 a night.

(189) Millie said that she is always asking the Duffers - usually to no avail - for a few more scenes in Stranger Things where Eleven actually gets to smile.

(190) Noah Schnapp said that Millie arranged for a Mariachi band to come in and play on his last day of shooting on Stranger Things 4

(191) You can now, should you desire, buy Stranger Things lipgloss.

(192) Millie seems to be fond of sunbathing if her photographs are anything to go by.

(193) Although she has been to some exotic places to shoot movies, Millie says it is not as glamorous as it sounds because you spend most of the time working and don't get

to relax or see as much of the place you are in as you might hope.

(194) The Duffer Brothers have always put parts of themselves in certain Stranger Things characters. They were both held back a year in school because of their refusal to mix with other children. The Duffers said that when they were in high school they used to eat their lunch together in the car to avoid the cliques and social interactions of the cafeteria. They previously included elements of their own teenage life in outsiders like Barb Holland and Jonathan Byers and do so again with Eleven (and perhaps even Eddie Munson too) in season four. The Duffers do not have fond memories of high school and this clearly manifests itself in the show.

(195) Millie is a fan of the film Booksmart. This is a comedy about two high school girls about to graduate.

(196) Millie likes the idea of being a director one day but thinks she has a lot more acting to do before that day arrives.

(197) 'Mouthbreather' - a term Eleven and the boys use in season one of Stranger Things - is slang for a stupid person or annoying person. If someone was getting on your nerves you might say - 'You are SUCH a mouthbreather'.

(198) Millie said she tried an electric hair drying cap during the lockdown. She didn't seem to be too impressed.

(199) As any Stranger Things fan worth their salt will already know, the show was originally going to be called Montauk and set by the coast. When these plans were abandoned they had to come up with a brand new title. The

titles they considered were The Rift, The Nether, Sentinel, Flickers, The Keep, The Tesseract, and Wormhole. The Keep was the title of a Michael Mann horror film and The Tesseract was the title of an Alex Garland novel so no prizes for originality of those two fronts (which probably explains why they were not chosen). A title they nearly settled on was Indigo but Matt Duffer eventually came up with Stranger Things - which was inspired by the Stephen King story Needful Things.

(200) The moment where Lucas shoots the Demogorgon in the Stranger Things season one finale with his wrist-rocket and it is thrown back (we quickly deduce that Eleven REALLY did this - not Lucas) is a riff on the scene in Saving Private Ryan where Tom Hanks fires a futile pistol shot at a tank just as the tank is about to be bombed by an aircraft. You might say then that in this instance Lucas was the distraction and Eleven was the heavy artillery.

(201) Millie is said to own a Cadillac Escalade.

(202) Henry Cavill, Millie's co-star in the Enola Holmes movies, auditioned to become James Bond in 2005 for Casino Royale. Henry was one of the final three candidates and apparently the preferred choice of director Martin Campbell but in the end the Bond producer Barbara Broccoli chose Daniel Craig. Henry was only 22 at the time and was ultimately felt to be a trifle too young to be 007 - even though the film actually depicted a younger Bond new to the secret service.

(203) You can buy a Magiclux 3D 'Illsuion' Stranger Things Figurine Lamp - which can emit seven different colours. You can choose either Eleven, Eddie Munson, or Dustin as the character depicted in the lamp.

(204) The Radio Times wrote of Enola Holmes 2 - 'What's heart-warming about this sequel is that the filmmakers have responded to audiences' love of Cavill and, of course, Sherlock himself by giving the character more screen time, but not at the expense of Brown's infinitely watchable Enola. The script beautifully juggles both Holmes siblings to ensure we get our fill of both, with Sherlock often baffled by the skills of his little sister and Enola giving good eye-roll as she realises Sherlock is a bit of a mess. Whether you figure out the finale or not, there are still enough well-directed carriage chases, stirring fight scenes and dynamic sleuthing to keep the blood pumping. And Millie Bobby Brown is, as always, an absolute pleasure to watch.'

(205) The Piggyback is the first Stranger Things season finale where Eleven and Mike do not kiss.

(206) It was reported in the media in 2022 that the 'kids' in Stranger Things were going to get $7 million each for season five. Millie's salary was a mystery though because it was part of a broader Netflix deal she'd signed earlier. Some media reports allege that Millie is in 'tier one' on the show when it comes to wages and will get the same as David Harbour and Winona Ryder - who are both allegedly going to be paid $9.5 million for Stranger Things 5. One entertainment site even alleged that Millie was going to get $20 million for Stranger Things 5 - which seems remarkable if true.

(207) The Duffer Brothers said they considered pulling The Lost Sister from Stranger Things 2 but decided to include it in the end. They acknowledged that - as fans of the show pointed out - The Lost Sister was a problem when it came to pacing in the season. Just as season two has gone into top gear the handbrake is applied and we have the detour of

The Lost Sister. Not to say that literally everyone hated the episode but, generally, it wasn't well received.

(208) Millie said it was a bit weird having to learn monologues and reams of lines for Enola Holmes because she was used to giving a largely non-verbal performance in Stranger Things.

(209) Millie says Melodrama by Lorde is one of her favourite albums.

(210) Millie said that on Stranger Things you are often on the set at 6am and don't get home until well into the evening. You also have to do some night shoots too. The exhausted actors often take a nap in their trailers while waiting for their scenes. Not that we should feel too sorry for them because they are lavishly paid for their labours!

(211) Fancasting sites have suggested that Millie should play Kitty Pryde in an X-Men movie. This role was previously played by Eliott Page.

(212) Millie said she once had a dream where she got the characters of Eleven and Enola Holmes hopelessly muddled up and kept ruining Stranger Things by making comical asides directly to the camera!

(213) Millie said that being home schooled was a trifle lonely at times but she has no regrets about not going to a regular school again after she left her primary school.

(214) Millie says she isn't a fussy eater and will eat virtually anything.

(215) Millie said that when she was ten years-old a casting

director made her cry by saying she would never make it as an actor.

(216) Stranger Things 4 required an incredible 300 days of shooting before it was in the can. Millie and the cast must have felt like they had been shooting it forever when they were finally allowed to depart and move onto other things.

(217) The diorama of Hopper's cabin that Eleven takes to school at the start of Stranger Things 4 is in a box for Reebok trainers/sneakers.

(218) In July 2022, Millie and Jake Bongiovi were photographed enjoying a holiday in Sardinia, Italy.

(219) Millie said she was very tearful when she finished her last scene on Stranger Things 4 because she knew the show would not last forever and they were now much closer to the end of Stranger Things than the beginning.

(220) Millie said she identifies with Enola Holmes a lot because they are both have a dry sense of humour and are sometimes too honest for their own good.

(221) Time Out wrote of Enola Holmes 2 - 'Out of all the hundreds of Netflix films, Enola Holmes feels the most like it belongs on the small screen. Its recreation of Victorian London – all music halls and grand saloons – looks a bit soundstagey; its sprawling cityscape suffers from an overload of CGI. But for an evening in, it's reliable entertainment. That's thanks mainly to Stranger Things' charismatic Millie Bobby Brown, whose charming, brilliant and surprisingly fighty sleuth steps out from the shadows of her more famous brother, Sherlock (Henry Cavill), in a sparky story of young feminists socking it to corrupt 19th

century gents and bent coppers.'

(222) Millie said she calls Mariah Carey by her nicknane of 'Mimi'.

(223) Eleven's dramatic return at the end of the Stranger Things 2 episode The Mind Flayer, where you see a slow motion shot of her footwear entering the besieged cabin at first, was a homage to a scene of Neo entering a building in The Matrix.

(224) A lot of the Stranger Things cast members say that it only really dawned on them that the show was a big thing and they were now famous when they saw action figures for sale with their likeness!

(225) Millie says that she tries to "unapologetically be herself" in her life.

(226) At the start of 2022, staff at a coffee shop in Bodmin, Cornwall were amazed when Millie and her boyfriend Jake Bongiovi dropped in a couple of times. The coffee shop is apparently quite famed for their waffles but given what we know about Millie it is highly unlikely that she ordered any!

(227) For the scenes in Stranger things 4 where Eleven is in the sensory deprivation chamber water tank they had to use an overhead Technocrane because it was impossible to put a camera in that sealed environment.

(228) Millie said her favourite scene in Stranger Things 4 is the one in The Monster and the Superhero where Eleven tearfully asks Mike Wheeler why he never puts 'love' at the end of any of the letters he writes to her.

(229) Millie said that it is a very curious and illogical phenomenon to get abuse online from people who have never even met you and have no idea what you are like in real life.

(230) Millie won the award for "Favorite Movie Actress" at the 2023 Kids' Choice Awards.

(231) Millie says she likes quiet places away from crowds of people and hustle and bustle.

(232) The makeup department on Stranger Things 3 complained when the catering department served Millie and the cast ice lollies during a warm spell. Lollies are a nightmare for the makeup people and continuity because all the actors are liable to end up with orange or yellow tongues after eating them.

(233) Millie said the other young cast members in Stranger Things are sort of like her cousins. They don't talk to each other constantly but they are always there for one other.

(234) In 2022, Millie posted snaps of her Christmas tree on Instagram on the 14th of November. The middle of November is probably a bit early for most of us to put our tree up!

(235) Urethane resins, rope, pool noodles and bubble wrap were used to create the icky vines of the Upside Down in Stranger Things 4. Millie (as Eleven) had to be wrapped in the vines later in the season.

(236) Believe it or not, you can now buy kitchen sponges made to look like Stranger Things VHS tapes.

(237) Millie says she helped to design the costumes on the Enola Holmes films.

(238) Eleven has spent more time crying than any other character in Stranger Things. There are over twenty episodes where Eleven cries.

(239) Millie has to have security staff now when she goes shopping. This is one of the downsides of fame. It is difficult to lead a normal life.

(240) There was speculation a few years ago that Millie was going to play Red Ranger in a new Power Rangers movie but this turned out to be nonsense. Mighty Morphin' Power Rangers was an Americanised version of the Japanese show Kyoryu Sentai Zyuranger. Millie's former Stranger Things co-star Dacre Montgomery actually starred in a Power Rangers movie himself.

(241) Despite a number of nominations, Millie and the cast members of Stranger Things were absent at the 2022 Emmys. It is believed that a combination of other commitments and a sense that they were not frontrunners to pick up many awards explained why no one from the show turned up.

(242) Millie is an advocate of Kombucha. Kombucha is a fermented, lightly effervescent, sweetened black tea drink commonly consumed for its purported health benefits.

(243) Eleven has a Bambi figurine on her desk in Stranger Things 4.

(244) Millie said it took her a while to get into the swing of Enola Holmes - where she was encouraged to improvise if

the mood took her - because everything is very scripted on Stranger Things.

(245) When Sullivan and the military storm the missile silo in the Stranger Things 4 episode Papa to capture Eleven this is a homage to the corridor sequence at the start of the original 1977 Star Wars.

(246) Millie said she became a vegetarian but lapsed because she didn't have enough energy or muscle mass on that diet.

(247) Eggo waffles only really became popular in the 1960s.

(248) Enola Holmes has a fresh 92% rating on Rotten Tomatoes at the time of writing. Variety wrote - 'The first film had a lightly contemporary political edge, situating Enola in a diversely cast world of parliamentary reformers and ass-kicking women's-rights activists. The new one goes even further: The capitalistic cruelty of the match factory makes an impression on Enola and on us; it's poignant that the person who's hired her to solve this case in the first place is Sarah's younger sister, Bessie (Serrana Su-Ling Bliss), herself a destitute match-factory girl without a penny to her name. But the movie also moves; it knows not to take itself too seriously, and never feels like a holier-than-thou lecture about the Bad Old Days. For all its narrative ornamentation and socially conscious grace notes, Enola Holmes 2 is still basically a kids' movie about a smart and plucky girl who solves crimes. And what kind of fussbudget could have a problem with that?'

(249) There were very vague plans to make Stranger Things as a found footage movie at a very early stage but the Duffers admitted that they didn't actually like found

footage movies much so this was a bit of a non starter. At the time the found footage genre was back in fashion thanks to the success of the Paranormal Activity movies. Found footage goes back decades as a subgenre of horror but it was The Blair witch Project which brought it to the mainstream and - for better or worse - inspired the deluge of found footage movies which have been released since 1999. The Blair Witch Project is a low-budget 1999 horror film directed by Daniel Myrick and Eduardo Sanchez. The film had a clever and innovative internet marketing campaign and became a box-office smash through good word of mouth despite its minuscule budget. The premise is simple and not entirely original. Three students - Heather Donahue, Joshua Leonard, and Michael C Williams - go hiking into the woods of Burkittsville, Maryland in 1994 to investigate and make a documentary film about a local legend known as the Blair Witch. They are never heard from again but the film they shot with their video equipment is recovered. This shaky footage reveals what happened to them in the Black Hills of Burkittsville.

(250) Millie has said that she isn't very good at running.

(251) Millie says she loves 'Scouse' accents. A Scouse accent is the accent that people from Liverpool have. Millie said she has tried to impersonate this accent but isn't very good.

(252) Stranger Things 4 began production under the secret codename Tareco. Tareco is a type of biscuit popular in parts of Brazil. The codename was obviously done to try and negate any spoilers. It is fairly common for highly anticipated films and TV shows to shoot under a secret codename as a means to (hopefully) throw the media off their trail. Stranger Things had been using secret codenames during production since the second season.

(253) Millie said she has gone to karaoke nights with Mariah Carey.

(254) PR 'guru' Mark Borkowski said of Millie - "Her success is partly what I call the Harry Potter effect and partly down to her ability to win over Gen Z with social media. It's that perfect storm of factors. Child stars that are part of a franchise like Harry Potter – and Stranger Things – are growing up in front of their fans who are on that journey with them, so they have this captive audience. Add to that all the older sci-fi fans and her fanbase is already large. It was once a curse to be a child star but now, with the right management and team around, it doesn't have to be, as Daniel Radcliffe and Emma Watson have both shown. Taking out a full page ad in a magazine no longer works for brands. They need to be able to bring in new, younger audiences to stay relevant and that's what Millie is able to do with them. To Gen Z she is completely relatable – she cares about the things they care about and has struggled with the same things."

(255) Though time is usually in short supply on a production as big as a season of Stranger Things, the Duffers will usually allow the actors to rehearse a scene a few hours before it is actually shot.

(256) Though she always seemed to dread the end of Stranger Things, Millie seems to have come to terms with the fact that the show can't go on forever and has said she is now excited about the 'next chapter' in her career after Stranger Things 5.

(257) Millie said she was sad about Billy's death in Stranger Things 3 because she loved working with Dacre Montgomery.

(258) Millie said she never has the faintest idea what is
going to happen in a new season of Stranger Things until
she turns up to start shooting it and gets her hands on some
scripts. The Duffers clearly keep their cards close to their
chest for fear of spoilers leaking.

(259) The Duffer Brothers said that, even when she was
still a little kid on season one of Stranger Things, Millie was
always quite bold in offering opinions on what her
character Eleven would or wouldn't do in a scene. The
Duffers said they like this because the characters become
more fleshed out when actors take ownership in this way.

(260) The first name of Enola Holmes was inspired by the
town of Enola, Pennsylvania, near where the author Nancy
Springer grew up

(261) Millie said she was pleasantly surprised by the
success of the Enola Holmes movies.

(262) Millie's tattoos are on her wrist, collarbone, back, and
ribcage.

(263) Millie said she is not a fan of the bowl haircut that
Noah Schnapp's character Will Byers has in Stranger
Things. Noah is no fan of this haircut either and has often
asked for it to be changed. Luckily for Noah it's only a wig.
He doesn't literally have to get a Dumb & Dumber/Bastian
Balthazar Bux haircut for the show.

(264) Millie went to both China and Japan to attend the
premieres of Godzilla: King of the Monsters in those two
nations. Godzilla is of course an icon of Japanese pop
culture.

(265) Millie has been seen dining at Don Angie. Don Angie is a Michelin starred modern Italian-American restaurant and bar in the West Village of New York.

(266) Millie attended a Harry Styles concert at Wembley Stadium in the summer of 2022. She went with Jake Bongiovi and Noah Schnapp.

(267) Paul Reiser's Dr Owens calls Eleven 'kiddo' in Stranger Things 4. This is what Reiser's character Carter Burke kept calling Sigourney Weaver's Ripley in Aliens.

(268) In 2021, Millie, as part of her partnership with Converse, selected 20-year-old Thai design student Pauline Wattanodom to help design a new range of the footwear

(269) Millie says that she finds housework and cleaning strangely therapeutic.

(270) Millie once got up on stage and rapped with Maroon 5 at a concert.

(271) Martie Blair had to have her long hair shaved off to play the nine year-old version of Eleven in Stranger Things 4. This is what Millie had to do too back in 2015 for the first season of the show.

(272) One of Millie's tattoos is the name 'Ruth'. This is the name of her late grandmother.

(273) Millie said she hardly saw David Harbour during the production of Stranger Things 4 because they only had one scene together at the end.

(274) Millie said she likes browsing YouTube to pass the

time. She said she gets quite obsessed by celebrity wedding videos.

(275) In 2017, Millie said she talks a lot to Cara Delevingne about fashion through text messages. Cara Delevingne is an actress and model about ten years Millie's senior.

(276) Millie said she was a bit worried that people might find Eleven less interesting in Stranger Things 4 because the character spends much of the season without her powers.

(277) As part of a W magazine piece in 2020 where celebrities dressed as a character from their favourite 'Quarantine' show, Millie dressed as Rachel (Jennifer Aniston's character) from Friends.

(278) Millie once said that she is quite envious of Gaten Matarazzo's luxurious Italian hair! Gaten, as you are well aware, plays Dustin Henderson in Stranger Things.

(279) Millie said if she's going to a function or formal event it usually takes her about 90 minutes to get ready.

(280) Millie said that she first read the Enola Holmes books when she was about thirteen. She never dreamed back then that she would play the character one day.

(281) Millie says she dabbles in tie-dying t-shirts. According to the Collins dictionary - 'If a piece of cloth or a garment is tie-dyed, it is tied in knots and then put into dye, so that some parts become more deeply coloured than others.' (282) When Eleven's life flashes before her eyes when Henry has the upper hand in the rainbow room battle in The Massacre at Hawkins Lab this seems a lot like a homage

to the trippy credits in the original 1978 Superman movie with Christopher Reeve.

(283) The eagle-eyed will notice that Eleven wears a ring in Stranger Things 4. This was presumably a gift from Mike when she left Hawkins at the end of season three.

(284) Millie said that her friends in England tend to call her 'Mil'.

(285) Millie wore velvet, sequins, and lace in a custom Louis Vuitton gown at the 2022 BAFTAS.

(286) Millie is the youngest ever collaborator with the Converse brand.

(287) Eleven at school in Stranger Things 4 clearly draws some inspiration from Stephen King's Carrie. Carrie White struggled to fit in at school too.

(288) The scrunchies worn by the female characters in Stranger Things are made by the costume department and designed to match the character's clothes.

(289) One of Millie's tattoos is a rose.

(290) It was dubiously reported in March 2023 that Millie had turned down $10 million to star in a Stranger Things spin-off movie. This was a clear example of what you would call fake news. The Duffers had already stated that they had no plans to do a spin-off with any characters from the base show. Entertainment sites love bogus stories like this because they get a lot of clicks as a consequence - hence the term 'clickbait'.

(291) Over the four seasons of Stranger Things, Millie as
Eleven still has more screentime than any other
actor/character in the show - clocking up over eight hours
of screentime. Dialogue is another matter entirely though as
Eleven is a girl of few words.

(292) It is probably fair to say that the Sherlock Holmes
played by Henry Cavill in the Enola Holmes movies is a lot
kinder and more sympathetic than the more aloof and stern
Sherlock Holmes depicted by Nancy Springer in the Enola
Holmes books.

(293) The Craft was mentioned by the writers as one of the
influences on Stranger Things 4. This is a 1996 film about
four teenage outcast girls who dabble in witchcraft to make
themselves more popular and get what they want but, as
ever in the horror genre, you should be careful what you
wish for. The Craft's central character Sarah Bailey moves
to California at the start of the film and finds it difficult to fit
in with the cliques and popularity contests of school and
girls of her own age. This theme was an influence on Eleven
in California in Stranger Things 4.

(294) Millie says she is bonded for life with the Stranger
Things cast members. They will always have that
connection from the show.

(295) Millie says the main reason why she's never
completely got into video games is that she simply doesn't
have the time to play them.

(296) Millie has grown very close to Sarah Hindsgall, the
Emmy-nominated head of the Stranger Things hairdressing
department. Millie has called Sarah her 'second mother' on
social media. Sarah Hindsgall has watched Millie grow up

on the set as she's known her since 2015.

(297) Millie thinks can do quite a good Australian impersonation.

(298) According to the net, if you want to hire Millie to give a speech at a function it will allegedly cost you $200,000.

(299) The first Enola Holmes film is largely based on the first book in the series, The Case of the Missing Marquess.

(300) In April 2022, images from the new edition of the Stranger Things Monopoly game appeared on social media and apparently sent the Duffers in a 'meltdown' because they divulged some secrets about the forthcoming fourth season. The Monopoly images revealed that Eleven has her short hair back and goes to a top secret desert lab, that Hopper escapes from prison on a snowmobile, and that Eddie stages an impromptu concert to ward off bats.

(301) Millie said the main reason she ended up binging the television show Friends a lot with her family during the lockdowns in that they were finding the news depressing and just wanted some light escapism which took them out of reality.

(302) When she was thirteen, Millie got a special gift from Kim Kardashian in the form of Kim's new range of fragrances.

(303) Millie wore a Louis Vuitton dress to the Stranger Things 4 premiere.

(304) Millie wore a Raisa Vanessa Fall corset top on Jimmy Fallon in 2022.

(305) Millie has joked that because of her love of coffee she has drunk half of Starbucks.

(306) Millie wore Sabina Bilenko Couture to celebrate her 18th birthday.

(307) Millie is not the first celebrity to study with Purdue University. George Peppard, star of the TV show The A-Team and film Breakfast at Tiffany's, was a graduate of Purdue. Neil Armstrong, the first person to walk on the moon, also studied at Purdue University.

(308) According her parents, the first word Millie ever said as a child was 'caca'. This is Spanish for poop.

(309) Millie wore a Helmut Lang outfit to the 2019 WWD Beauty Inc Awards.

(310) Millie naturally attended the London premiere for Godzilla: King Of The Monsters.

(311) Millie said she lied about her age to open a Facebook account when she was six.

(312) Millie attended the Paris premiere for Godzilla: King of the Monsters.

(313) Millie also attended the Los Angeles premiere for Godzilla: King Of The Monsters. It seems she was contracted to attend literally every premiere for this film!

(314) Millie wore a Markarian Spring 2020 floral dress to a screening of Stranger Things 3 in New York.

(315) Millie said that her favorite Spice Girl was Posh Spice

(Victoria Beckham).

(316) Millie says she goes to therapy sessions - which have been a help in dealing with fame.

(317) Millie said she will always watch the film Mean Girls when it's on television.

(318) Because she has so many animals Millie said she spends a lot of time at the vets getting them checked out.

(319) Millie says a lot of her week is taken up with dog grooming.

(320) A fun but improbable fan theory is that Stranger Things takes place in the same universe as Stephen King's books. One problem with this theory is that we've seen characters in the show reading Stephen King books. The trooper that Hopper punches in the morgue in season one was reading Cujo and Lucas is reading The Talisman to Max at the end of season four.

(321) Stranger Things costume designer Kimberly Adams-Galligan created 'mood boards' to design the clothes each character wears in season one. Mood boards are basically sketches and illustrations of the characters so that the costume designers can get a clear picture of what they are going to look like in the show.

(322) Millie owns some bow front lilac Christian Louboutin 'Araborda' sandals.

(323) Millie said she named her tortoises after characters from Game of Thrones.

(324) Millie does not google herself but the one exception she made was when she was nominated for an Emmy. She couldn't resist taking a peek to read about that.

(325) Millie said she didn't especially enjoy working in the desert on Stranger Things 4. She said it was a bit too hot and dusty for her liking.

(326) D.A.R.Y.L. is a film playing at the Starcourt Mall in Stranger Things 3. This is a 1985 sci-fi fantasy film for children about a family who adopt a little boy but discover he's a sophisticated experiment in artificial intelligence. The government are after him and want to return him to a military facility (where his powers will be of use for espionage and computer hacking). The plot of D.A.R.Y.L. is quite similar to Eleven's arc in season one of Stranger Things. When asked about D.A.R.Y.L. at the time of season one, the Duffers said they had never heard of it. Perhaps this reference in Stranger Things 3 was their way of telling us they know about the film now? The little boy in D.A.R.Y.L. is played by Barret Oliver. Oliver also played Bastian Balthazar Bux in The NeverEnding Story. If you were casting Stranger Things in the 1980s then Barret Oliver would have made a good Will Byers or Mike Wheeler. Oliver stopped acting in 1989 and later became an artist and printer.

(327) When they were shooting the first Enola Holmes movie, Millie's family had her co-star Louis Partridge over as a guest at their roast dinner.

(328) The names of Millie's mum and dad are Kelly and Robert.

(329) An early fan theory in Stranger Things was that

Eleven is really Hopper's biological daughter Sarah. This theory was quite popular when people were watching season one but it seems to have a number of flaws which would be difficult to explain. Hopper seems to have no past with Terry Ives - who is clearly established by the show as Eleven's mother. If Hopper let the lab have custody of the ill Sarah to save her life, why is it that Hopper and Dr Brenner don't seem to know each other when they meet near the end of season one? If they do know each other, why doesn't Hopper ask to see Brenner when he investigates the lab? Also, wouldn't Eleven recognise and remember Hopper if he was her real father? One other detail (for the eagle eyed) is that Sarah and Eleven have different eye colours.

(330) Millie seems to be a fan of the short-form video hosting service TikTok.

(331) Millie said that her dad, much to her exasperation, still finds it funny to photo bomb her photographs.

(332) There has long been a Stranger Things fan theory that the Mind Flayer is really 001 from the Hawkins Lab. Stranger Things 4 more or less proves that this theory was correct all along.

(333) A website once opined that Millie's Enola Holmes performance is like watching a young Keira Knightley crossed with Phoebe Waller-Bridge.

(334) Millie said that she loves Meringue. Meringue is a dessert made from whipped egg whites and sugar.

(335) Stranger Things 4 shows us how Eleven escaped from the lab in season one because we see in 1979 that the orderly 'Peter Ballard' showed Eleven a storm drain exit in

the facility. This is what Eleven used to escape in 1983.

(336) Millie is a fan of the actress Jenna Ortega.

(337) Henry Cavill said of Millie - "She is both a sixteen-year-old and a 35-year-old at the same time. And she flip-flops between the two at her whim." Henry said that Millie would discuss acting in a mature serious way and suddenly flip into a typical teenager being all silly and singing songs.

(338) The episode of Modern Family that Millie appeared in was called "Closet? You'll Love it". She played a little girl who has her bike stolen.

(339) Eleven is designed to look like a mini-Joyce Byers at the start of Stranger Things 4.

(340) Stranger Things 4 generated 5.9 billion minutes viewed during the week of June 27, 2022.

(341) Millie is friends with the grown up children of Steve Irwin and spent some time with them when she was in Australia. Steve Irwin was a zookeeper, conservationist, television personality, wildlife expert, and environmentalist. Irwin became world famous for appearing in a host of animal themed television shows. He loved animals from a young age and devoted his life to teaching us more about them. Steve Irwin was a natural performer on television with his cheerful personality and trademark khaki outfits. Irwin was sort of like a real life Crocodile Dundee. He made cameos in Hollywood movies and was a frequent guest on the big American chat shows. Irwin's wife Terri was also involved in their shows and the couple had two children. Steve Irwin was building a huge franchise with his animal themed shows and

documentaries. He was arguably (with the possible exception of Mel Gibson - who is billed as American anyway in most places) the most famous Australian person in the world by the time of his death. On September the 4th, 2006, the 44 year-old Irwin was shooting a documentary titled Ocean's Deadliest in Queensland. Steve was fatally attacked by a stingray while shooting in the Great Barrier Reef and sadly died. It was just a very unexpected tragic attack that no one could have forseen. The Irwin family legacy lives on through his children - who both work with animals and so have continued the family's association with the animal kingdom.

(342) Millie has said that her siblings are not Stranger Things fanatics in the slightest and know surprisingly little about the show.

(343) Millie appeared on El Hormiguero in 2018. This is a Spanish comedy show with a live audience. She spoofed her Eleven character in a skit set on a train.

(344) Millie said that on Godzilla: King of the Monsters they once had to do 75 takes for one scene. This was very different from her experience on Stranger Things - where she was used to only doing a couple of takes for many scenes.

(345) Millie said that one of her biggest thrills was when she got to speak to Meryl Streep backstage at a chat show. Meryl Streep is one of the most acclaimed actors in Hollywood history.

(346) Millie said she enjoys playing Monopoly with her family.

(347) Millie said she would find it hard to get through the day without eating some chocolate spread.

(348) Hopper and Eleven's cabin in Stranger Things 3 seems intentionally designed to look like the cabin in Evil Dead II.

(349) Millie said that reading has never been her 'thing' and she hasn't read that many books. She said that, in mitigation, she does spend a lot of her time reading scripts - which makes it difficult to find the time to read books.

(350) Millie said that Friends star David Schwimmer once gave her some good advice when he told her that she should only do projects she is interested in and enthusiastic about because that way she'll always love her job as an actor.

(351) Millie said she got a bit of cabin fever during the pandemic and missed not going to work.

(352) When they designed the sound for the Upside Down in Stranger Things the sound designers used recordings of trees creaking in the forest in order to get that discordant and strange background aura.

(353) The retro Reebok sneakers Millie wears as Eleven in Stranger Things 3 were exceptionally hard to find and eventually purchased by the costume department at a vintage Atlanta market.

(354) Millie said she is usually happy to sign autographs and pose for a picture because fame comes with her job. She does feel though that it becomes intrusive if someone approaches her while she is out having dinner with her

family or boyfriend because this is private time.

(355) Millie said she would happily describe herself as 'woke'. Woke generally means someone who is 'politically and socially aware'.

(356) Millie said that growing up in the public eye was definitely strange and difficult at times because you feel as if you are constantly being watched and judged by everyone.

(357) There have been some Enola Holmes graphic novels. Enola is not illustrated to look like Millie.

(358) Millie thinks that when it comes to Eleven and Dr Brenner in Stranger Things, Eleven has developed a serious case of Stockholm Syndrome. Stockholm Syndrome is a condition in which hostages develop an unhealthy psychological bond with their captors.

(359) Millie said that she doesn't like watching herself in things she has acted in. A lot of actors seem to say this. It must be weird to watch yourself on the screen.

(360) When Millie met first Emma Watson at an awards show, Hugh Jackman was seated at the same table as Emma. This was a bit of a coincidence as Millie had unsuccessfully auditioned to be in Hugh Jackman's film Logan a few years before.

(361) Millie said she doesn't really have that many friends. She said she has a close circle of a handful of people.
(362) Millie said that the world of child acting was a very dog eat dog business. When you go up for a part as a kid the competition is fierce and there are hundreds of children all

going for the same role.

(363) Millie said that when she went for auditions as an aspiring child actor she always did bags of research so she knew all about the company or director she was auditioning for.

(364) Millie said it is important to have some friends who aren't in the entertainment industry because hanging out with 'normal' people keeps you grounded.

(365) 250 wigs were used during the production of Stranger Things 4. All the main characters have to have at least two wigs lest one should be damaged.

(366) Millie has joked that she wants Noah Schnapp to be the maid of honour at her wedding.

(367) Millie is a fan of the actor Jake Gyllenhaal.

(368) Millie said that when she was a little kid she would keep switching accents from English to American when she was in fast food places merely to amuse herself and confuse the person taking the order.

(369) The Duffer Brothers say that the Stranger Things spin-off show will not feature established characters like Eleven or be a Steve/Dustin show (a popular fan suggestion) because they feel like they've covered all of that in the base show and would simply be repeating themselves.

(370) Millie attended a basketball match between the New Orleans Pelicans and the Atlanta Hawks in 2022. She said she'd never been to a basketball game before.

(371) Millie said she had to start work on Enola Holmes 2 only two days after finishing her scenes for Stranger Things 4.

(372) Millie said her Stranger Things co-stars are awful at trying to impersonate her English accent.

(373) Millie said she once cheated on a test when she was home schooled.

(374) Millie said that making Enola Holmes 2 was especially nice because most of her family were often on the set with her.

(375) Millie has been to a Taylor Swift concert with her boyfriend.

(376) Fashion magazines have noted that Millie never really had that awkward teenage fashion phase which would make her look back and cringe because from a young age she had stylists and designer clothes.

(377) Millie said that it doesn't especially bother her that she missed out on traditional teen things like school and parties.

(378) Amazingly, once Eleven has her season one buzzcut again in Stranger Things 4, Millie suddenly seems much younger and looks uncannily similar to how she did in 2016 at times.

(379) Stranger Things is so popular that some industry observers wonder how Netflix will cope when it ends. The streaming service enjoys a big spike in subscriptions when a new season of Stranger Things is imminent so the loss of

revenue will be felt. They will simply have to hope that equally popular shows will emerge.

(380) Millie said she could speak some Spanish as a little kid but lost that ability when the family moved back to England.

(381) The California setting for Eleven's arc in Stranger Things 4 was very appealing to the Duffers because it would allow them to give the show some of its most overt Spielberg riffs yet - and that was saying something because Strange Things is rife with Spielberg riffs from the first season onwards. Spielberg's classic movies usually take place in planned communities near the desert. This is because that's where Spielberg grew up himself.

(382) In the film Damsel, Millie will play Princess Elodie. Elodie believes she is marrying a Prince but they really plan to sacrifice her to a dragon. Suffice to say, Princess Elodie intends to foil these dastardly plans.

(383) The Byers family moving to California in Stranger Things 4 somewhat riffs on the Emerson family moving to Santa Mira, California in the cultish 1987 vampire comedy The Lost Boys.

(384) May, 2021 saw the release of a Stranger Things 4 teaser trailer titled 'Eleven, are you listening?' It was unusual for the show to drip feed little trailers far in advance of the main show but simply a consequence of the marathon and delayed production of season four. They obviously felt the need to give fans a few crumbs while they endured the long wait to watch the new season. One could, at a stretch, note though that Stranger Things 3 DID have a similar teaser far in advance. In July 2018, the first teaser

for Stranger Things 3 arrived in the form of a fake (but remarkably period accurate and convincing) Starcourt Mall infomercial. At the end we got to see Steve and Robin in their Scoops Ahoy uniforms. A display in the mall during the teaser gave us a very a very brief glimpse of the Tom Clancy novel The Hunt for Red October. This was a big clue that the Russians were coming to season three. The teaser was rather frustrating for Stranger Things fans because they still had a year to wait before they could actually watch the new episodes.

Though fans didn't know it at the time, they would also have to wait a year to watch Stranger Things 4 after the 'Eleven, are you listening? teaser'! The teaser began with a ticking clock striking three and the ominous eye of a surveillance camera. Children in hospital style clothes chase toy cars across a rainbow pattern on the floor. Children are seen doing IQ tests and playing chess. The numbers 356 are shown and a man strides down a corridor before saying good morning to the children. Good morning Papa, they reply. Yes, this naturally Dr Brenner in what is obviously a flashback to yesteryear in the lab. Brenner says he has something special planned today. The teaser cuts a room with the number 11 on the door. No prizes for guessing which test subject lives in this room.

(385) The question of what a hypothetical Eleven spin-off show would even be about is a not inconsiderable conundrum. It would be rather difficult to do a prequel because Millie would be in her twenties by the time such a show went into production. The show would presumably have to take place outside of Hawkins because the other regulars were unlikely to feature. This is one of the obvious problems of a spin-off show. You'd miss seeing all the regular characters. Such a concept could work if the new

characters were memorable but it would obviously be very difficult to come up with a spin-off concept that didn't struggle under the large shadow cast by the main show. These were all the very reasons why the Duffers had no interest in such a show. After several years of Stranger Things you also couldn't blame them for wanting to do something different anyway.

(386) Gaten Matarazzo said that when they were shooting season one of Stranger Things there were a few comical mishaps with the long antenna on the walkie-talkies. He said Millie in particular got clobbered a few times by accident.

(387) Millie did a special UNICEF YouTube video for World Children's Day. The video had cameos by Liam Neeson, Dua Lipa, and Orlando Bloom.

(388) Online beauty discovery platform Cosmetify named Millie's make-up range Florence by Mills as one of hottest beauty brands of 2022.

(389) The Florence by Mills brand has branched out into clothing.

(390) The Enola Holmes/Viscount Tewkesbury relationship is known as "Holmesbury" by fans who 'ship' this duo. The dictionary definition of 'ship' in this context is 'to take an interest in or hope for a romantic relationship between (fictional characters or famous people).'

(391) The Stranger Things comics have always been told by Netflix they can never use the test subject 001 at the Hawkins Lab for a story. This was obviously because the Duffers planned to use the character on the show

themselves one day - as we saw in season four.

(392) There was once a Stranger Things fan theory that Dr Brenner was actually test subject 001 at the Hawkins Lab. This theory proposed that Brenner actually had some sort of special abilities or powers himself (though we hadn't seen them on display in the show). The source of this theory was the fact that Brenner never seemed to be scared of Eleven - despite the fact that she was highly powerful and even dangerous. Could it be that the reason why Brenner was unflinching in the presence of this Jean Grey style super child was the fact that he had similar powers himself? It seems as if this (rather interesting) theory turned out to be bogus.

(393) According to business sites, Florence by Mills makes about $2 million a year. The company is seen as one that is still expanding.

(394) It is estimated that Millie only had dialogue for about three minutes of Eleven's total screentime in season one. Eleven has more screentime (about sixty minutes) than anyone in season one so this is pretty remarkable.

(395) Florence by Mills is aimed at an under 24 demographic. The key with this demographic is that they want eco friendly and cruelty free products.

(396) Stranger Things: The Experience' - an immersive experience based on the show - opened in a number of cities in 2022. In the experience you get to rescue Max from Vecna and can also visit Family Video and Scoops Ahoy. The experience has drawn positive reviews in the media.

(397) When they designed the look of the Upside Down in

Stranger Things the production design team spent a lot of time researching mildew and the microscopic photography of organisms.

(398) Beach House Group was the group that launched the Florence by Mills brand. It was reported in 2020 that Millie had purchased a majority stake in Florence by Mills. This basically means she is now more or less the boss.

(399) Enola Holmes is something of a master of disguise. She takes after her brother Sherlock in this regard.

(400) The signature colour for the Florence by Mills brand is lavender.

(401) It was apparently Millie who had the idea of Enola Holmes speaking directly to the camera - a la Fleabag.

(402) Millie says that candles are essential when she has a bath. She likes to create a relaxing atmosphere.

(403) The wrap party for The Electric State movie took place at Your 3rd Spot, a new social dining experience located at The Works development in Atlanta's Upper Westside. The cast munched on smoked wild mushroom bruschetta at a private party and then enjoyed the games, cocktail lounge, and arcade offered by Your 3rd Spot. Millie was apparently seen doing some bowling on the bowling lanes.

(404) In September, 2022, Millie and Jake Bongiovi were seen visiting the Universal theme park in California. Media pictures showed that (doubtless among many other attractions) they went on a Star Wars ride.
(405) Millie owns some transparent green sunglasses.

(406) Millie and Jake Bongiovi were pictured enjoying a break in Barcelona in May 2022.

(407) When the titles for Stranger Things 4 were released, The Nina Project was (wrongly as it turned out) assumed by many to be a reference to a woman named Nina Kulagina. Nina Kulagina served in the Red Army during the Second World War and claimed to have psychic powers. She took part in many experiments in the Soviet Union in order to prove that her powers were real. Sceptics in the West though believe that she was a fraud used for Soviet propaganda and her powers were merely tricks and sleight of hand.

(408) Eleven's leg injury in Stranger Things 3 was written into the show after Millie injured her kneecap in real life.

(409) Millie wore a champagne coloured dress to the premiere of Stranger Things way back in 2016.

(410) Millie has announced that her debut novel, titled Nineteen Steps, will be available to buy soon. It is based on her own family history and set during World War 2. On her Instagram she said - "I'm thrilled to be announcing my debut novel, Nineteen Steps, which will be publishing on 12th September 2023. Nineteen Steps is a historical novel about an amazing, courageous 18-year-old woman called Nellie Morris, who lives with her family in Bethnal Green, in London's East End, while the second world war rages on around them. When a tragic accident occurs during an air raid one night, the consequences are catastrophic - and life will never be the same again for Nellie. Writing Nineteen Steps has been a really special project for me. The story is inspired by true events and my own family history. I really hope you will find the true spirit of love and strength in

Nineteen Steps, and I can't wait to share it with you."

(411) Millie has done Jiu-Jitsu from a young age so this helped for the fight scenes in Enola Holmes. She did say though that Jiu-Jitsu is rather more difficult to perform in a Victorian corset and heels!

(412) Millie said she like a good lasanga.

(413) Millie is sometimes known as 'MBB' on entertainment sites. It's a form of shorthand really.

(414) When the first Enola Holmes film was released, Millie recreated some of the trailer for a TikTok video.

(415) Millie and the other Stranger Things kids appeared on Carpool Karaoke! with James Corden in 2020.

(416) Stranger Things 4 was budgeted at a staggering $30 million an episode. This dwarfed the budget on season one - which was comparatively modest at around eight million an episode.

(417) Millie seems to like ice cream sundaes a lot if her social media is anything to go by.

(418) Though some of her Stranger Things co-stars have appeared on Broadway, Millie doesn't think she is ready yet herself to appear in a play or a musical show.

(419) Even though she didn't actually get the part, Millie said that her test for the part of X-23 in Logan was the best audition she ever did.

(420) The Duffers always loved the horror concept of some

fearsome entity who can't be explained. Pennywise and Freddy Krueger were certainly in this category. The villain Vecna in Stranger Things 4 was designed along similar lines in that it can play tricks on people and make them question what is real and what is not.

(421) Millie wore a Smocked Belted Jacket for an appearance on The Tonight Show. This jacket will apparently set you back over $4000 should you want to buy one.

(422) Millie wore a Target Ugly Holiday Snowman Long Sleeve Graphic Dress when she posed by her Christmas tree in 2020.

(423) Millie said that when she's in England she has fish and chips on Friday night.

(424) Millie thinks that her failed auditions when she was starting out as a child actor made her a stronger person because everyone has to overcome some setbacks and disappointment in their life but continue to move forward in the hope that things will get better.

(425) Millie said she still writes in her journal each day. Maybe in the far flung future these journals might form the basis of a memoir?

(426) Millie said she likes cat eye sunglasses.

(427) Those who know Millie usually say she is wise beyond her years. This is amply evident in the way she has built a business and commercial empire in conjunction with her acting/producing career - all while still in her teens.

(428) There seem to be some Catcher in the Rye references in Stranger Things. The Catcher in the Rye is a famous 1951 novel by J. D Salinger. The first reference comes during the memorial to Will Byers in the school in season one when Mike calls some of the people who have - despite hardly knowing Will - turned up 'phonies' - a term that Holden Caulfield uses frequently in The Catcher in the Rye. In season two there seems to be another Catcher reference when Eleven is a fugitive in the woods and sports a hunting hat she took from a hunter. Holden wears a red hunting hat in the book, which he turns backwards.

(429) In their 2014 review of the TV show Intruders, The Hollywood Reporter called Millie's performance 'phenomenal'.

(430) One of Millie's directors on the TV show Intruders was Eduardo Sánchez - who co-directed The Blair Witch Project.

(431) In their 2014 review of Intruders, Variety wrote - 'Very X-Files-ish in tone (and featuring some prominent alums of that show among its producers), Intruders is another moody, macabre drama that proves too stingy about disgorging its secrets. Adapted from Michael Marshall Smith's novel, the series involves, as the press notes explain, "a secret society devoted to chasing immortality by seeking refuge in the bodies of others," without really making clear the rules through two rather violent episodes. Fans of the genre might be more patient about where this serialized story is heading, but those confined to one lifetime should think twice before potentially squandering some of it on this.'

(432) Stranger Things casting director Carmen Cuba said of

casting Millie in the show - "As herself, she was a bright, shining light of a kid filled with enthusiasm about playing and being imaginative, but in the role she could shut that off and go really deep and intense. Having a kid who was naturally similar to Eleven in darkness and intensity would have been hard, because nobody wanted to feel like we were torturing someone so young and still developing emotionally."

(433) Millie's salary on Enola Holmes 2 was higher than Robert Downey Jr, Matt Damon, and Emily Blunt got for appearing in the next Christopher Nolan movie.

(434) Though her $10 million salary on Enola Holmes 2 was lavish, Millie still has a long way to go to catch up with the big male stars in Hollywood. Actors like Dwayne Johnson and Brad Pitt command a salary of about $30 million a film. Tom Cruise earned $100 million for Top Gun: Maverick.

(435) Randy Havens, who plays the science teacher Mr Clarke in Stranger Things, said he was astonished by how good Millie and other kids were in season one.

(436) Millie said she likes to drizzle Marmite over the top of a roast dinner as a final touch.

(437) Millie said that when she was growing up the clothes she wore to functions and premieres had to be approved not just by her parents but her entire team.

(438) Millie said in the past she would be up for an appearance in Henry Cavill's show The Witcher. Henry has since left the show so this offer may not stand anymore.

(439) Millie said that on the set of Enola Holmes she has fun

trying to annoy Henry Cavill by endlessly talking about things he has no interest in - like reality television and Taylor Swift songs.

(440) Millie said she would love to be fluent in Spanish but she just hasn't found the time to learn the language.

(441) Millie said that Enola Holmes is a very special role to her because it was the first time she was ever the lead in anything.

(442) Though she was born in Spain and spent a lot of of her life in America, Millie has always had British citizenship through her parents.

(443) Millie is very hopeful that there will be an Enola Holmes 3.

(444) If her social media pictures are anything to go by Millie seems to love lakes and rivers.

(445) Millie is often encouraged to sing at convention appearances. Not that she needs much encouragement to do so!

(446) Millie said that nothing bothered her when she was a little kid but she started to suffer from anxiety when she was about fifteen. Fame was obviously a salient factor in this.

(447) Millie, as you might presume, supports England when it comes to international football.

(448) Millie was once interviewed by Drew Barrymore. Drew Barrymore was in Spielberg's E.T when she was a kid.

This film was a big influence on the first season of Stranger Things.

(449) Millie said she is very difficult to embarrass and so rarely suffers from embarrassment.

(450) Millie has, tongue-in-cheek perhaps, suggested that the Duffers should kill off more characters in Stranger Things so the cast isn't so big.

(451) Although he plays the oldest (and stuffiest) Holmes sibling Mycroft in Enola Holmes, in real life Sam Clafin is actually three years younger than Henry Cavill.

(452) Millie's favourite type of milkshake is strawberry.

(453) Millie said it was quite emotional shooting her last scenes with Matthew ('Papa') Modine in Stranger Things 4. Millie first worked with Matthew when she was about eleven years-old so they've developed a close bond.

(454) Millie has a rather arduous pre-production on the Enola Holmes movies because not only is she a producer she also has to do extensive stunt training.

(455) Millie used to want Nancy to end up with Steve in Stranger Things but she's changed her mind about this and now wants Nancy to end up with Jonathan.

(456) A few years ago, a 'stylist to the stars' compared Millie to 1960s model Twiggy. What he presumably meant was that both were hip, British, and slender!

(457) Millie said that her way of decompressing from the celebrity life has always been to play Barbie dolls with her

younger sister.

(458) Despite her commercial deals and business dabblings, the vast majority of Millie's net wealth was accrued through her acting career.

(459) Millie has been known to sport a beanie style hat when she is trying to go incognito.

(460) The only one of the kid characters in Stranger Things who never met Dr Brenner in person is Max.

(461) The Millennium Falcon toy that Eleven levitates in season one of Stranger Things is specifically the 1980 Empire Strikes Back Millennium Falcon reissue from Kenner Toys.

(462) When they have to depict blood in a character's mouth (or even near their mouth) in Stranger Things, the makeup department uses a fake blood mixture that is made up of dried cranberries, black cherry Jell-O mix, Emergen-C powder, and some water. Emergen-C is a powdered vitamin supplement.

(463) Millie and her boyfriend have been photographed being allowed to enter a club or nightspot through the back entrance. One of the perks of fame is that you don't have to wait in line!

(464) Millie will be an executive producer on her new Netflix movie Damsel - in addition to starring in the film.

(465) Millie did a 'Spicy Wings Hot Ones' challenge in 2022. She did not appear to enjoy the experience too much.

(466) Helena Bonham Carter's agent apparently advised her not to do the first Enola Holmes movie because it was a relatively small part.

(467) Millie has been asked what she thinks of the American accents done by other British actors in films and shows but she was too diplomatic to answer the question.

(468) Millie is a fan of the actor Tom Holland.

(469) One could argue that the makers of the TV show Intruders are somewhat under publicised in Millie's story because they discovered her two years before Stranger Things even came out.

(470) As long as they aren't preposterously hot, Millie quite likes eating raw chillis.

(471) Millie called Finn Wolfhard a 'lousy' kisser in 2022 while doing a lie detector test for YouTube. Finn took this comical insult with good humour.

(472) Millie said that when she was a child actor the only way to cope with the rejections was to understand that you aren't suited to every part you go for.

(473) The episode of Grey's Anatomy that Millie appeared in was called "I Feel the Earth Move". In the episode, Millie played a little girl who phones the hospital after her mother takes a fall during an earthquake!

(474) The episode of NICS that Millie appeared in was called 'Parental Guidance Suggested'. Millie was just ten years when she appeared in this show.

(475) Millie said she has an insect named after her in Australia - courtesy of the Irwins.

(476) Millie is a fan of the television show Euphoria.

(477) Millie wore some Christian Dior Lime tartan tailored trousers for one of her Enola Holmes 2 interviews.

(478) Millie said that Stranger Things coming to an end is sort of like leaving school and saying goodbye to people you've grown-up with.

(479) A lot of people have said that Millie looks like a very young Elizabeth Perkins. Elizabeth Perkins is probably best known for her role in the Tom Hanks film Big.

(480) Millie sometimes refers to her friend Noah Schnapp as 'Schnipper' on social media.

(481) Millie cancelled a convention appearance around the time she was shooting Stranger Things 2 because she was too exhausted to attend.

(482) Millie's favourite water brand is Fiji.

(483) Millie once said that her favourite smell was vanilla.

(484) Millie is partial to an acai bowl. Acai bowls are made from acai berries and often additional fruits, then topped with ingredients like fruit, nuts, seeds, and granola.

(485) Millie said that Netflix often remind the cast members of Stranger Things to be aware of divulging spoilers. They have to be very careful in particular about what they post or say on social media - especially during shooting.

(486) Millie said her spirit animal is the Orca. These are also known as killer whales. Despite this name these whales are friendly unless threatened and have even come to the aid of humans being attacked by sharks.

(487) Millie said she was lucky in that she always wanted to be an actor and got a chance to do this. Many people grow up without a clear idea of what they want to do.

(488) Millie said she thinks she has generally been a good daughter to her parents.

(489) Millie said she is amazed at how Stranger Things appeals to all ages. She has met people her grandparents age who love the show and kids even younger than her who love the show.

(490) Leigh-Anne Pinnock, Perrie Edwards and Jade Thirlwall from Little Mix attended the bash for Millie's 16th birthday.

(491) Millie's Enola Holmes co-star Louis Partridge said she sometimes telephones him in the middle of the night and wakes him up because she completely forgets she's in America and there's a big time difference when you call someone in England!

(492) Millie said her favourite season is Winter.

(493) There is a rather obvious parallel between Millie and Enola Holmes in that both were educated at home.

(494) Millie said her favourite superhero is Princess Leia. I suppose you could say Princess Leia IS a superhero because she has Jedi mind powers.

(495) Millie was seen chatting with Henry Winkler at the 2020 SAG Awards. Winkler has been in many things but is best known for playing the 'Fonz' in the sitcom Happy Days.

(496) Millie is a fan of the children's film Matilda.

(497) A play based on Stranger Things titled Stranger Things: The First Shadow is due in 2023. The new play is written by Stranger Things TV series writer and co-executive producer Kate Trefry and directed by The Crown's Stephen Daldry with co-director Prima Facie's Justin Martin.

(498) Millie said she got a sore neck shooting Godzilla: King of the Monsters because she constantly had to look up to pretend she was gazing up at the giant Godzilla!

(499) Millie said she was rather sad to hear that the Kardashians were ending their reality show.

(500) Millie's Enola Holmes co-star Louis Partridge said she had McDonald's fast food delivered most days while shooting.

(501) Millie said she got the part of Eleven in Stranger Things one day after doing a screentest in Los Angeles. Prior to this she had done some Skype auditions from England.

(502) Millie said that she had to cry during one of her Stranger Things auditions and thinks her ability to turn on the pretend watwerworks might actually have bagged her the part of Eleven.

(503) The walkie-talkies that Eleven and the boys use in

season one of Stranger Things were purchased at a Long Beach flea market by the prop master Lynda Reiss.

(504) Louis Partridge said that Millie ate a ridiculous amount of carrots while they were shooting the Enola Holmes movies.

(505) In a YouTube video, Millie said she had a couple of birthmarks on her back and under her arm.

(506) The mouth and the head of the Demogorgon in Stranger Things somewhat resembles a Rafflesia arnoldi. Rafflesia arnoldii, the corpse flower or giant padma, is a species of flowering plant in the parasitic genus Rafflesia.

(507) Brown is the sixth most common surname in Britain. According to Wikipedia - 'Most occurrences of the name Brown are derived from a nickname concerning the complexion of an individual, the colour of their hair or the clothing worn. This nickname is derived from the Old English brun, brun; Middle English brun, broun; or Old French brun.'

(508) Millie has joked that she is tempted to get a Leonardo DiCaprio tattoo.

(509) Millie thinks she looked like a 'little potato' in the first season of Stranger Things.

(510) Ross Duffer said that in an ideal world they would have shot Stranger Things 4 and Stranger Things 5 back to back so it could have just carried on straight on and the younger actors would all have looked exactly the same in both seasons but this was simply not practical. As a consequence of this there will be a time jump between the

seasons.

Given that it needed 300 days of shooting and months of post-production to get Stranger Things 4 completed the notion of making two seasons back to back was clearly ludicrous. The digital effects alone would have taken months and months to finish. There is also the fact that the actors have other professional commitments too. It would be impossible to tie down Millie or David Harbour for two years because these actors are constantly being offered movies. Last but by no means least, shooting two seasons of the show back to back would have placed a preposterous workload on the Duffer Brothers. How would they have found any time to write the scripts for the last season?

(511) Millie said that New York is beginning to feel like a second home now because she has been there so many times to do interviews.

(512) Millie said she picked up a fair bit of Victorian slang from making the Enola Holmes films.

(513) At one point Millie made six television appearances inside 48 hours to promote Stranger Things 2 in 2017.

(514) When she was named one of the 30 Most Influential Teens of 2017 by Time, the magazine wrote - 'Not many actors can say they got an Emmy nomination, and worldwide fame, for convincing the world that they have superpowers. Brown can, thanks to her role on Netflix's sci-fi '80s-nostalgia-fest Stranger Things. She plays Eleven, a mysterious girl—part science experiment, part prodigy, part awkward teen—who uses telekinesis to ward off evil. But there's remarkable nuance in Brown's performance, the kind that is able to convey melancholy beneath magic. It has

made Eleven the standout character on a show brimming
with them, one who inspires Internet memes, Halloween
costumes and newfound interest in Eggo waffles (Eleven's
favorite food). Brown's own profile has risen as well. Since
the show's July 2016 debut, the British actor has rapped at
the Golden Globes, signed with IMG Models and appeared
on the covers of Entertainment Weekly, InStyle and more.
One secret to Brown's success? Not overthinking her craft.
"Eleven is part of me and always will be. I don't try with
her," she told TIME during a Stranger Things set visit earlier
this year. "I don't even know my lines for today's scene ...
and that's what makes it so instinctual."'

(515) Millie said that her greatest crisis during Stranger
Things 2 came when she developed an annoying pimple on
her ear! Happily, this pesky pimple was eventually
vanquished.

(516) While it was nice to have a solo spotlight on Eleven
and Millie was - as usual - very good, The Lost Sister
episode in Stranger Things 2 felt a lot like an experiment
which didn't quite come off. It was as if the Duffer Brothers
were testing the waters to see if episodes outside of
Hawkins were viable in the show going forward.

(517) Millie (as Eleven) has only been absent from two
episodes of Stranger Things. The two episodes are The Spy
and Dear Billy.

(518) Millie said that the idea of going to a school and
sitting in a class with 20 other kids didn't appeal to her in
the slightest.

(519) Gaten Matarazzo said that Millie was very shy when
he first met her at the Stranger Things auditions.

(520) Millie said she only got to see and talk to the Duffer Brothers about three weeks after her first Skype audition for Stranger Things.

(521) Millie wore a Miu Miu military jacket for a 2017 fashion shoot in Australia.

(522) Millie said her older sister was very excited when she appeared in Grey's Anatomy because she was a fan of the show.

(523) The Duffers cut quite a lot of scenes out of the famous bike chase sequence (where Eleven throws the lab van up in the air with her powers) in season one of Stranger Things because they wanted it to be punchier and more fast paced.

(524) Millie said it was very exciting to meet John Travolta at a function. Millie loves musical films and John Travolta was famously the male lead in Grease.

(525) The Roller King in Albuquerque was shut down for a month to become the 1986 Rink O Mania (where Eleven whacks Angela with a roller-skate) in Stranger Things 4.

(526) In 2017, Millie was interviewed by Evan Rachel Wood - who was one of the stars of the HBO show Westworld. Millie had to confess that she hadn't seen Westworld because her parents felt she wasn't old enough to watch it!

(527) The eerie chime of a grandfather clock which heralds Vecna's arrival was also used in season one of Stranger Things 4 for the arrival of the Demogorgon. The production team said that they purchased four vintage grandfather clocks to use in Stranger Things 4.

(528) The sequence where Eleven takes out Brenner's agents in spectacular (if grisly) fashion in the school corridor during the season one Stranger Things finale is the most obvious example of the influence on Eleven of the character of Lucy from the manga Elfin Lied. Both Lucy and Eleven escape from a laboratory and have amazing powers. The main difference is the use of violence. Lucy is known for gruesome blood soaked kills. Eleven in Stranger Things is not so ferocious or cold blooded and Stranger Things - naturally - is not as violent or gore caked as a Japanese manga. The school corridor scene is a rare case though of Eleven at her most extreme. She is willing to do anything to escape. It is the closest we get to manga Eleven.

(529) Millie has been seen dining at the Chiltern Firehouse. The Chiltern Firehouse is a restaurant and hotel located at 1 Chiltern Street, Marylebone, London. The Firehouse is a well known celebrity hangout place.

(530) When they were hired to compose the music for Stranger Things, one of the first tasks that Kyle Dixon and Michael Stein were given by the Duffers was to pitch demo themes for Eleven and the other child characters in the show. The Duffers knew that Dixon and Stein could do moody and electronic but they need to know that the composers could also do sad and even whimsical too.

(531) For her nineteenth birthday, Millie had dinner at the Beauty & Essex Los Angeles restaurant on North Cahuenga Boulevard in Los Angeles. This is described as - 'A sophisticated, jewel-toned eatery with vintage decor offering New American plates, drinks & wine.'

(532) Stranger Things makeup department head Amy L. Forsythe said that for the infection wounds in season three

on Eleven and other characters she researched the effect of animal bites on human skin and then replicated this with the use of mannequin legs to refine the makeup effects. Amy said she got some rather bemused and baffled looks from her team at first when she asked them to go out and buy her some mannequins.

(533) The acronym for Hawkins Power and Light, the cover name for the secret government agency controlling Eleven in season one of Stranger Things, is HPL. This is a reference to the famous horror author H.P. Lovecraft. Lovecraft's stories are often about inexplicable creatures, alternate dimensions, and forces we can't possibly understand.

(534) The xx's Romy Croft said of Millie (after Millie appeared in their music video) - "Millie is absolutely so intelligent and quick and really lovely, and came up to everyone and was really warm. She was singing the song on set, so I thought that was a good sign. It was connecting with her, and everyone was really sweet."

(535) Millie had never seen any of the old Japanese Godzilla movies when she was cast in Godzilla: King of the Monsters.

(536) Vecna's hands in Stranger Things 4 contain creepy extra long clawed fingers. Mechanical metal finger extensions were specially built to add to the Vecna suit by the prosthetics team.

(537) Millie was seen sporting some zebra print flared trousers in 2023.

(538) When the third season of Stranger Things was released, an entertainment website complained that the subtitles made too much use of the words "squelching" and

"squelch" in relation to the Mind Flayer's body horror shenanigans!

(539) Millie said she noticed she was being recognised by strangers for the first time about three days after the first season of Stranger Things dropped on Netflix.

(540) The idea of sensory deprivation tanks is that you are removed from all external stimuli as a means to explore the nature of human consciousness. Sensory deprivation tanks obviously play a big part in Stranger Things.

(541) President Obama apparently binged Stranger Things on his plane Air Force One in preparation for meeting Millie and some of the cast and crew at the White House.

(542) Millie says that, much to her dismay, she has never quite mastered doing the cartwheel.

(543) Millie seems to be quite fond of oversized bomber jackets.

(544) Production on Stranger Things 4 went two months over schedule - which would probably partly explain why fans had to wait so long for it to be released. What with the pandemic hiatus, a range of shooting locations, and billions of digital effects, it is little wonder that we had to wait so long for Stranger Things 4.

(545) Film Stories said of Enola Holmes 2 in their review - 'The plot does have a few too many rug-pulls scattered throughout though, so the conclusion doesn't quite have the 'aha!' moment of the best mystery stories, but there's enough humour and fun little word puzzles along the way that the action never gets dull. It's helpful, of course, that

Millie Bobby Brown, who also produces the film, is there to drag the movie along by its Victorian coattails. The first film was reportedly a real passion-project of hers, and in the second she ramps up the considerable charm she already displayed in her last outing. Her heroine is wonderfully expressive, and a huge amount of credit for the film has to go to her lead performance. The only downside is that Henry Cavill, returning as Enola's slightly more famous older brother, seems a bit dull by comparison, though that Bobby-Brown's star power manages to outshine Superman himself is surely something to go right at the top of her CV.'

(546) Millie said that when she got caught up in the whirl of crazy celebrity fame through Stranger Things her older siblings were very good in keeping her feet on the ground and making sure she got enough to eat and plenty of sleep.

(547) The Critic's Slant website reviewed the marketing campaign for the first Enola Holmes film and concluded - 'The campaign is just a lot of fun. With Enola breaking the fourth wall to share her thoughts and frustrations with the audience, her attempts to break away from the path her brothers and society would like her to follow and her determination to find her mother, a great sense of humor and attitude permeates the various marketing assets on display here. The trailer is great, but the posters are also very important in establishing the movie's brand for the audience. How the designs evoke the poppiest of pop culture, reminiscent of movies like Sofia Coppola's Marie Antoinette, which had the same attitude on display. More than all that, it's a chance for Brown to really breakout from her breakout role and show the kind of range she's capable of.'

(548) Millie insisted on doing her own fights and stunts in

Enola Holmes because she enjoyed the challenge and it also made it more realistic for the audience to see that the lead actor was in the thick of the action (as opposed to a stunt double).

(549) Millie's sister Paige is a producer on the Enola Holmes films. In fact, it was Paige who first read the books and felt they would be a good vehicle for Millie. Millie said she and Paige never have any creative disagreements and get on really well.

(550) In the first Enola Holmes film they rationed the use of the colour red so that Enola's red dress would be more striking and set her apart from her surroundings.

(551) The first Enola Holmes film made use of Benthall Hall in Shropshire. Apparently, they got permission to film there because the daughter of the caretaker was a big fan of the Enola Holmes books!

(552) Millie's collaboration with Vogue Eyewear included eight different frames inspired by her favorite cities.

(553) Kyle Chandler, who played the father of Millie's character in Godzilla: King of the Monsters, said of her - "She's a kid, and she's a cool kid. She's got a great curiosity and she likes to study what she does so she knows her craft. She's a pretty interesting young person in the business. I think you'll see a lot of her do a lot of different things in the future."

(554) Matthew Modine said that during a break on the production of Stranger Things 4 he went on a day trip with the kids in the show and ate some dog biscuits intended for Millie's dog by mistake!

(555) Beyond the Black Rainbow is a rather obscure Canadian science fiction horror film written and directed by Panos Cosmatos. Beyond the Black Rainbow is set in 1983 and takes place at a research facility called the Arboria Institute. The facility is investigating the mind and its connection to science and stimuli. They seek to explore sensory therapy in a new age of enlightenment. Dr Barry Nyle (Michael Rogers) seems to be one of the few scientists left in the facility and is keeping a young woman named Elena (Eva Allan) captive in the depths of the laboratory. Elena has psychic powers and communicates through telepathy. She eventually tries to escape.

Beyond the Black Rainbow is a bizarre film and an enjoyably surreal experience. Several years later when Stranger Things became a huge success, film buffs who had watched Beyond the Black Rainbow noticed some interesting similarities between Stranger Things and this little known movie. Both are set in 1983. The telepathic girl's name (Elena) is close to Eleven. After she escapes from the lab, Elena nervously explores in the woods just as Eleven does in the first episode of Stranger Things.

Beyond the Black Rainbow also has a synth music score that sounds similar to the one in Stranger Things. There is even a 'vat' scene in Beyond the Black Rainbow that unavoidably reminds one of the sensory deprivation tank in Stranger Things. Both Elena and Eleven kill their captors with mind powers and television (as a means of entertainment and vessel of communication) is vital to both characters. Dr Barry Nyle is rather similar to Matthew Modine's Dr Brenner in both his treatment of and fascination with his telepathic subject. As an experience in its own right though, Beyond the Black Rainbow is beautifully strange and full of incredible imagery. This is rather like some strange unknown science fiction film that you'd find in an eighties video store. Beyond the Black Rainbow is not the most coherent film you'll ever watch but it is a rewarding and interesting experience. If you love Stranger Things, watch Beyond the Black Rainbow and see what you think of all the alleged similarities.

(556) Millie said she decided to take the online college course in human services so that she is better equipped to help young people.

(557) Millie visited Universal Studios Orlando's Halloween Horror Nights with her boyfriend in 2022.

(558) The Electric State was based in Atlanta for much of its production so Millie certainly would have felt at home given that Stranger Things is also based there and she has a house in Georgia.

(559) Millie seems to be fond of hammocks.

(560) According to Deadline, Millie was paid $2 million for Stranger Things 3. This was a huge pay increase from the first season - where Millie is believed to have earned about $160,000.

(561) Millie said that 1990s supermodels like Naomi Campbell, Tyra Banks, and Kate Moss were an inspiration for her fashion and makeup.

(562) Millie is obviously a fake blonde. She went back to her usual dark brown hair when shooting on The Electric State was over.

(563) Millie bested Jimmy Fallon on a 'beat battle' karaoke

game on The Tonight Show in 2019. The songs she sang
were - Carly Rae Jepsen's "Call Me Maybe," Lorde's "Royals,"
Gwen Stefani's "Hollaback Girl," Shawn Mendes' "If I Can't
Have You," Lizzo's "Juice," Panic! at the Disco's "High Hopes"
and Zedd, Maren Morris and Grey's "The Middle."

(564) Millie's height is (at the time of writing) believed to
be about 5'6. It seems safe to presume that she isn't going
to get too much taller.

(565) Because she was born in February, Millie's 'Life Path'
number in Numerology is actually 9. Numerology (known
prior to the 20th century as arithmancy) is the belief in an
occult, divine or mystical relationship between a number
and one or more coinciding events.

(566) There seem to be a few snide YouTube videos and
articles which claim that Millie is rude and has become a
diva. The evidence presented for this though is vague to say
the least. People who know Millie think she has navigated
incredible and insane fame at a ridiculously young age as
well as anyone could reasonably have hoped and remained
a down to earth and decent person.

(567) Millie seems to have been quite savvy and selective in
choosing her roles outside of Stranger Things. She appears
to pick personal projects and parts that are right for her
(one could obviously argue that the Godzilla movies were
less personal and simply chosen for commercial reasons)
rather than just do any old rubbish that comes her way.

(568) During the production of Stranger Things 4, Matthew
Modine was a guest of Millie's family and ended up staying
for three months! He lived in the guest house.

(569) One of Millie's social media videos seemed to show that she has a Marilyn Monroe poster on the wall.

(570) Millie had some sparkler candles on her nineteenth birthday cake.

(571) Millie seems to be friendly with the actress and singer Teala Dunn.

(572) Millie seems to pout a lot in her photographs these days. Maybe she doesn't even realise she's doing it!

(573) Making the film Damsel was no picnic for Millie because she had to do an awful lot of stunts and fights.

(574) Millie's early roles were unusually dark. She played a little girl inhabited by a serial killer, a girl who killed her mother, and then of course Eleven - a monosyllabic girl held captive by the military. No wonder she enjoyed flexing those underused comic acting chops in Enola Holmes!

(575) The famous board game Dungeons & Dragons plays a big role in Stranger Things. While several members of the cast (most notably David Harbour and Finn Wolfhard) are fans of this game in real life, Millie has never displayed any interest in it herself.

(576) Although she didn't have any scenes with him, Millie said she loved Joseph Quinn's performance as Eddie Munson in Stranger Things 4.

(577) The characters in Stranger Things all have their own arcs and quests. They all develop. Hopper is world weary and slobbish when we first meet him but the search for Will Byers brings forth all the good qualities that he had hidden

deep inside. Dedication, bravery, selflessness, kindness. Nancy goes from vacuous teen to warrior. Steve goes from absolute douche to hero. Eleven goes from victim to protector. And so on.

(578) The Duffer Brothers said that, when they were trying to pitch and sell Stranger Things, one network executive advised them to get rid of the horror elements and adult characters and just make it as a children's mystery show. It's safe to say that this executive didn't understand what the Duffers were trying to do. Thankfully they ignored his advice.

(579) Millie said that when she first went to Los Angeles she used to walk past famous theatres and cinemas used for glitzy premieres and dream of attending her own premiere one day. Her wish came true in the end.

(580) Millie has done some social media posts in support of the Black Lives Matter movement.

(581) Gaten Matarazzo said he wanted to get Millie on his Netflix show Prank Encounters but this obviously never transpired in the end. Prank Encounters is sort of like a supernatural themed Candid Camera.

(582) Stranger Things makeup artist Amy L. Forsythe said she came up with her own backstory concerning who did Eleven's makeup for the Snow Ball dance in Stranger Things 2. Amy said that Hopper would obviously have no clue about makeup and so probably asked Nancy. Nancy, in turn, probably borrowed some makeup from her mother Karen. This then, in a circuitous way, provides a perfectly logical explanation for why Eleven has purple eyeshadow at the Snow Ball!

(583) Millie said she thought that shaving her head for Stranger Things might be a waste of time because she didn't expect the show to be very big.

(584) Millie said she is not scared of snakes. She even put one around her neck when she was in Australia.

(585) Millie and the Stranger Things youngsters were often seen at Six flags amusement park in Georgia when early seasons of Stranger Things were in production. This theme park is only a twenty minute drive from Atlanta. Six flags amusement park now has a spooky Stranger Things maze.

(586) The scene at the end of The Mind Flayer in Stranger Things 2 when Eleven dramatically returns is a partial riff on the scene in Alien: Resurrection where Winona Ryder's android character Call is suddenly revealed again - despite apparently just dying.

(587) The clothes that Eleven rejects during the mall montage of Eleven and Max together at the mall in Stranger Things 3 were the actual clothes that costume designer Amy Parris and Millie rejected when they were testing clothes for Eleven to wear in season three.

(588) Millie said that she reads new scripts every single day.

(589) Millie said when she was very little she wanted to be a singer but then she got the acting bug and so that all changed.

(590) Bella Ramsey, the girl who beat Millie to a part in Game of Thrones, is now becoming a pretty big star thanks to her role as Elle in the HBO show (adapted from a video

game) The Last of Us. This all has a strange sort of symmetry because The Last of Us (the video game that is) was an influence on Stranger Things and many think that Elle inspired Eleven's name - which is usually shortened to 'El' by her friends.

(591) The Starcourt Mall in Stranger Things 3 is really Gwinnett Place Mall in Atlanta. This mall opened in 1984 but eventually fell on hard times and was pretty derelict when the Stranger Things production team found it. Netflix leased about 20% of the mall and completely renovated it - putting in the facades of around forty 1980s period authentic stores. They also installed an operational food court. Millie and the kids had fun at this mall - although they do think it was haunted.

(592) Millie seems to be a fan of Amina Muaddi shoes.

(593) The Duffer Brothers said that 99% of child actors would not have been capable of fronting a big dramatic show in the way that Millie, Finn, Gaten, Caleb, and Noah did in season one of Stranger Things.

(594) The kids in Stranger Things like to decorate their trailers when a new season is in production.

(595) Millie seems to be quite fond of sporting ripped jeans.

(596) Millie is a fan of the fashion designer Tabitha Simmons.

(597) Millie was seen wearing Air Force 1 Trainers in 2020. These are apparently quite rare.

(598) Millie said that before Stranger Things she had to do

any acting job she was offered. Now she can pick and choose.

(599) In the original pitch for Stranger Things (still titled Montauk at the time), the first season was going to be set in 1980. The Duffers proposed that a second season would take place in 1990 - ten years later. The idea here was obviously that the kids would have to meet up again as young adults a decade later and fight the evil infecting Hawkins again. This was inspired by the structure of Stephen King's IT. The problem with this idea is that all the kids would have had to be recast in season two. That concept quickly became unthinkable.

(600) Millie said she would love to work with Matthew Modine again one day in something else when Stranger Things ends.

(601) How did Mr and Mrs Wheeler not notice that Mike had Eleven secretly living in the laundry room in season one of Stranger Things? Well, Ted probably wouldn't notice anything at all so that's understandable with but what about Karen? The Duffer Brothers said that Karen didn't notice Eleven because the basement is Mike's private domain for D&D and toys so she never goes down there.

(602) The name of the talent manager who first discovered Millie is Melanie Greene.

(603) Millie's dad used to be an estate agent in England.

(604) Notice how the music score stops and there is silence during the big van flip stunt by Eleven in the Stranger Things episode The Bathtub. This tactic by the composers is very effective.

(605) When Eleven is in the void in season one of Stranger Things and reaches out to touch the Demogorgon it seems to be crouching over an egg or even maybe feeding on it. This is never really explained.

(606) Millie was remarkably articulate and relaxed for one so young in her first interviews when she became famous at the age of twelve.

(607) Millie is quite often seen out attending pop concerts in Atlanta.

(608) Millie's house in Atlanta has a white picket fence around the garden.

(609) Stranger Things: Six is a comic which revolves around Francine - who is a test subject at Brenner's lab named SIX and has the ability to see the future. She has visions of the Demogorgon and waffles. The waffle visions definitely baffle and irritate Dr Brenner because they seem meaningless. Anyway, Six plans to escape from the lab and wants to take some other patients with her - especially two twin sisters. This is a fairly readable comic with not bad art and an interesting story. Eleven makes a brief appearance (this is set before the events of season one) and we see Brenner introduce the big sensory deprivation water chamber to the lab. You'd probably say that this is one of the best Stranger Things comics because it feels quite ambitious and because this is a prequel it doesn't feel too constricted by having to tiptoe around the actual TV show in the way that other Stranger Things comics tend to do.

(610) Millie has homes in London and Atlanta but it is believed she also rents a house in Los Angeles.

(611) In 2020, Millie was seen attending an Atlanta United game. Atlanta United FC, commonly known as Atlanta United, is an American professional soccer club based in Atlanta that competes in Major League Soccer (MLS).

(612) Millie has been seen several times at Black Tap Craft Burgers & Beer in the Soho area of New York. She usually orders a milkshake.

(613) According to the website Digital Trends, Stranger Things 4 is the most popular (as in most streamed) Netflix show (or season in this specific case) of all time - edging out Wednesday and Dahmer. Stranger Things 3 was in sixth place.

(614) Millie has blinds in her bedroom.

(615) Millie said her greatest wish is that all children in the world are happy, safe, fed, and educated.

(616) Millie said when Noah Schnapp got stuck in a chair shooting Stranger Things 2 that rather than lend assistance she decided to film it on her phone!

(617) Millie said she loves Henry Cavill's red Ducati motorcycle. The sensible and safety conscious Henry was adamant though that he wouldn't take her for a spin on it.

(618) Millie had to learn how to ride a Victorian style bicycle for Enola Holmes. Bikes back then had one wheel bigger than the other.

(619) The highest rated episode of Stranger Things on IMDB is The Massacre at Hawkins Lab with 9.6.

(620) The production of the first season of Stranger Things was incredibly low-key in hindsight. There was practically no coverage when it began shooting and hardly any promotion when it was due to be released. Many members of the cast presumed the show would fly under the radar and quickly be forgotten (which would obviously have kiboshed any hope of a second season). In a sense then one can see how shrewd Netflix executives were in their approach. They were confident that the show was good and would have a lot of mainstream appeal so they worked on the basis that good word of mouth would propel the show to success. In the end this is exactly what happened.

(621) One of the people who does the subtitles for Stranger Things said that using the words 'tentacles undulating moistly' to describe the sound effects of Vecna in his lair was done as a bit of a joke.

(622) According to national records in Britain, female babies being named Millie spiked after Stranger Things came out in 2016. They then spiked again in 2021 when Millie Court won Love Island. So, in short, Stranger Things and Love Island are responsible for an awful lot of kids being named Millie!

(623) Millie owns a pair of pink slippers from Justin Bieber's own fashion line Drew House.

(624) Millie wore a Lacy Blush Gown at the Godzilla: King of the Monsters premiere in London.

(625) Nicolas Ghesquière put a runway model in a Stranger Things t-shirt for Louis Vuitton in 2017. Millie is strongly associated with this brand.

(626) Notice how at the end of the Stranger Things 4 episode The Nina Project that Brenner, as in season one, seems completely unconcerned about the poor security guards who now lay in a crumpled and inert heap thanks to Eleven!

(627) Millie said that she started going to the gym to do boxing and Jiu-Jitsu in London when she was a kid because she was a bit lonely and bored as a homeschooled child and wanted something to do.

(628) It has been suggested that there is a possible contradiction in the 1979 lab scenes in Stranger Things 4 that the 1979 version of Eleven seems more articulate and fluent when speaking than the 1983 version of Eleven did in season one. This is forgetting though that the 1983 version of Eleven was deeply affected by the events of 1979. Besides, it's not as if the 1979 version of Eleven was very chatty either. She's more or less the same Eleven we saw in season one.

(629) Millie was seen wearing burgundy Dr Martens boots in London in 2019.

(630) Seasons one, two and three all have three episodes in the top ten highest rated Stranger Things episodes on IMDB. Stranger Things 3, by contrast, only has one episode in the top ten - the season finale The Battle of Starcourt. This would suggest that IMDB voters tended to feel that season three wasn't as consistently strong as the other seasons.

(631) The device used in the lab by Brenner in Stranger Things 4 to inhibit Henry Creel's powers in the 1979 lab flashbacks is called a soteria. In Greek mythology, Soteria

was the goddess or spirit (daimon) of safety and salvation, deliverance, and preservation from harm. Eleven is duped into removing this device and so must then battle Henry.

(632) Millie became a Two Stripe BJJ White Belt in Jiu-Jitsu in 2016.

(633) The children in Brenner's 1979 lab in Stranger things 4 all seem to have more or less the same sort of abilities as Eleven - which is slightly odd because in season two we met Kali/008 and her powers of hallucination.

(634) Caleb McLaughlin, Sadie Sink, and Gaten Matarazzo all vaguely knew each other before Stranger Things because they had worked on Broadway and the stage and their paths had crossed. None of them had ever met Millie before though.

(635) You can, should you desire, now buy a life-sized cardboard cut-out of Millie.

(636) Millie has gone out for Chinese food with Mariah Carey.

(637) Millie's boyfriend Jake Bongiovi was a good athlete in high school and played American Football.

(638) It was reported in 2022 that Florence By Mills was the most googled and social media engaged beauty site. Millie's association and campaigning obviously had a lot to do with this.

(639) The manufacturing base for Florence By Mills products is apparently El Segundo, California.

(640) Millie says that when she has a 'cheat day' with food and wants a guilty pleasure she will usually have a burger and fries.

(641) Millie does circuit training in her workouts. This includes some jumping jacks and weights.

(642) Millie still does Muay Thai training. Muay Thai is basically kickboxing.

(643) Millie said she often had lunch with her brother while making Enola Holmes 2. The film was very much a family affair on the set.

(644) Millie said the wig she wore in Stranger Things 4 left her with some pimples and blemishes on the front of her head - which then had to be covered up when she went straight into shooting Enola Holmes 2.

(645) The two episodes of Once Upon A Time in Wonderland that Millie appeared in as the young Alice when she was a little kid were titled Down the Rabbit Hole and Heart of Stone.

(646) Once Upon a Time in Wonderland was a spin-off from the show Once Upon a Time. Once Upon a Time ran to seven seasons but Once Upon a Time in Wonderland was axed after one season. These shows were - of course - based on Alice's Adventures in Wonderland and Through the Looking Glass.

Alice's Adventures in Wonderland was published in 1865 and written by Lewis Carroll. Lewis Carroll was the pseudonym of Charles Dodgson. Dodgson was also a scholar, poet, and mathematician. He conjured up the adventures of Alice as a means to entertain the children of some friends during lazy summer days by the river. Once his fantastical tales were put into book form, Alice's Adventures in Wonderland eventually became of the most famous and enduring works of fiction ever published.

 The book concerns a young girl named Alice who is dreamily sitting by a riverbank when she notices a white rabbit race past. Nothing strange about that you might think. However, this rabbit is wearing clothes and seems to keep checking a stopwatch as if time is of exceptional importance at this precise moment. Alice, naturally curious about this remarkable sight, explores but falls a down a rabbit hole into a strange world full of remarkable creatures who seem somewhat like the animals and insects of our world - only they can talk. It quickly transpires that logic plays little part in this topsy turvy and endlessly eccentric and strange world. But is it all a dream or is Alice really here?

Curiously, Alice's Adventures in Wonderland was not very well received when it first appeared and it was only after the publication of the sequel (Through the Looking Glass) that it got some traction and become much more loved and widely read. It's hard really to think of many more influential books than Alice's Adventures in Wonderland. It has inspired dozens of film and television adaptations and the image of little Alice in her blue dress is as identifiable as any character in fiction. Alice's Adventures in Wonderland is a delight on every page and fantastically weird and offbeat. The book is a wonderful celebration of nonsense and whimsy and full of preposterous conversations, memorable characters, puzzles, poems, and enjoyable absurdity. One can more or less include the sequel Through the Looking Glass in any discussion of Alice's Adventures in

Wonderland as these two books are equally strong and equally delightful. Through the Looking Glass has a similar sort of premise (in the sequel Alice explores the world that exists on the other side of a mirror) and is more of the same really with classic characters, puzzles, absurdist humour, and an enjoyable disdain for convention or reality. These two books remain great fun for children but are also recommended to any adults who (for whatever reason) simply never got around to reading them.

(647) In 2022, Millie said of the Duffer Brothers - "They gave me an opportunity that not many people were giving me at the time. They believed in me, and they knew I was capable of something. I'm just very grateful, and they've always been there for me."

(648) Millie has now worked for two different sets of brothers - the Duffers for Stranger Things and the Russos for The Electric State.

(649) Millie said that when she got an Emmy nomination at the age of thirteen she was too young to actually realise the significance of this.

(650) Millie had to wear a leg brace when she injured her knee in 2019.

(651) Before its release, there was a bogus theory that Eleven might turn bad in Stranger Things 4 and be a villain. When asked about this, Millie said that while it would be fun to play a baddie but she wouldn't want Eleven's character to change in any drastic way. It is probably safe to say that the Duffers are highly unlikely to turn Eleven into the villain of Stranger Things!

(652) Millie said she built up a huge collection of face masks during the pandemic. She got ones in all different colours.

(653) During the production of Stranger Things 4, David Harbour set up an Instagram live from his trailer and (jokingly) threatened to reveal a load of spoilers. Millie interrupted his live feed and told him to stop talking about the show!

(654) It is probably true to say that the Brenner/Eleven backstory in Stranger Things 4 contradicts a lot of the Stranger Things comics and novels. It is probably best just to think of these as different entities.

(655) Millie said she likes some stuffing with her roast dinner. Stuffing is made from - among other things - herbs, onions, and breadcrumbs.

(656) Millie said is is quite difficult to relate to Eleven because she has so little in common with the character. Eleven is a telekinetic super powered girl who was raised in a military scientific facility so it would be rather difficult for anyone to relate to this!

(657) Millie said that film and television sets are nearly as exciting as you might think and she often takes naps during breaks.

(658) Millie purchased a Akubra bushman hat the first time she went to Australia.

(659) Millie is sometimes reported to have dated Romeo Beckham - though Millie said they were just friends. Romeo Beckham is one of the children of David and Victoria (aka Posh Spice) Beckham. Romeo is a footballer now - though

soccer superstardom seems rather unlikely as he is already 20 and on loan to Brentford's B team.

(660) Millie said she got quite emotional when she first watched Godzilla: King of the Monsters and saw her name on the credits. To be in a big film fufilled an ambition.

(661) Millie said that when she was homeschooled and juggling this with acting she did tend to end up doing her school work late at night.

(662) Millie once said that she would like to own a property in the south of France.

(663) The day that Millie was born (February 19th, 2004), Slow Jamz by Twista & Kanye West was on top of the singles charts in America, camera phones were still a relative novelty, and Tony Blair was the Prime Minister of Britain. The big films that month were The Passion of the Christ, 50 First Dates, and Barbershop 2: Back in Business.

(664) In December 2022, Millie posted a picture on social media of her and Jake Bongiovi scuba diving.

(665) Millie says that her beauty care range is based around hydration.

(666) Millie is allowed to have input into the clothes that Eleven wears in Stranger Things.

(667) The end of Enola Holmes 2 introduces Dr Watson. In the story it is Enola who engineers for Sherlock to have a roomate.

(668) There is a big distinction between what Millie wears

in normal life and what she wears for interviews and premieres. In real life she obviously doesn't swan around in designer dresses 24 hours a day.

(669) Millie said one of the worst things about growing up in the spotlight is the sense that people are waiting for you to make a mistake.

(670) Millie has yet to do a purely dramatic role but that seems sure to come. One could actually argue that her part in NICS is the straightest performance she has given. She has plenty of dramatic scenes in Stranger Things but that show is fantastical in nature with plenty of sci-fi, horror, and comedy.

(671) There is obviously a bit of a contradiction in Millie's environmental statements in that she seems to eat meat, like fast food outlets, and spend a lot of time on planes. These are all things that environmentalists should really seek to avoid.

(672) The Enola Holmes films are essentially comedic escapism but that specific era does allow for some political and social commentary. Social injustice was rife, poverty was all too common, and women were fighting for the right to vote.

(673) It is slightly odd that Millie seems to dislike strawberry ice cream but love strawberry milkshakes!

(674) Millie said she grates raw carrots before she eats them. You probably wouldn't want to eat the dirt and rough bits on the outside!

(675) Millie washes her dogs in the sink.

(676) Many reviews of Kong vs Godzilla seemed to find Millie's character rather superfluous. It's probably fair to say that this film wasn't the best use of her talents. Most viewers were only there to watch Godzilla fight a giant ape anyway!

(677) Millie said the film Damsel was right up her alley because the film is about a young woman who refuses to accept the role allocated to her by society. The societal role in this case is that of a human sacrifice to a dragon!

(678) Millie said she will always regard Stranger Things with fondness and affection because it was her big break and a huge part of her formative years.

(679) Millie said she got a 'therapy' dog on her 16th birthday on the advice of Miley Cyrus.

(680) Millie seems to be more light-hearted in her interviews these days. In fact, her twelve year self actually seemed more serious back when Stranger Things first came out!

(681) Millie's English accent is definitely becoming a trifle on the Transatlantic side at times after those years in America.

(682) The 'kids' in Stranger Things don't seem to be interviewed in a big group all together as they were in the old days. They tend to split the cast up more for interviews now.

(683) Millie said that when she goes food shopping she will inevitably head for the cookie/biscuit section first.

(684) Millie was very dogged in her pursuit of the Enola Holmes rights because she knew this character would finally give her a chance to flex her comedic chops. All actors, even teenage ones, are wary of being typecast.

(685) Assuming her money is invested wisely, Millie is already financially secure for life. That will doubly be the case when her bumper fee for Stranger Things 5 is banked.

(686) Though she clearly loves her grub, Millie seems to be one of those people who never puts on weight. All that exercise clearly helps in this regard.

(687) Millie says that drinking water usually perks her up when she's low on energy.

(688) Millie is a fan of Arcade Dance Machines.

(689) When Eleven takes out the army helicopter in the Stranger Things 4 episode Papa this feels a lot like a nod to the Kryptonian supervillain Ursa toying with the army helicopter in Superman II.

(690) Millie's friend Noah Schnapp launched his own vegan chocolate hazelnut spread in 2022. As a fan of chocolate spread, Millie has doubtless sampled this.

(691) Colonel Sullivan's obsession with Eleven is somewhat on the vague side in Stranger Things 4 in terms of his motivation but we do see that he seems to connect the deaths in Hawkins (at the hands of Vecna) with the gruesome deaths of Connie Frazier and the government agents in the school corridor (which happened in the season one finale). Sullivan therefore seems to believe that Eleven ALONE is responsible for all of these strange and

harrowing deaths.

(692) Millie is a big fan of the song Party in the U.S.A by Miley Cyrus.

(693) Millie seems to be a big fan of wearing slippers at home.

(694) Millie visited the La Sagrada Familia when she took a break in Barcelona. The Basílica i Temple Expiatori de la Sagrada Família, shortened as the Sagrada Família, is the largest unfinished Catholic church in the world.

(695) Millie and her boyfriend were seen at the Rockefeller Center near the end of 2021. The Rockefeller Center is a large complex consisting of 19 commercial buildings covering 22 acres between 48th Street and 51st Street in the Midtown Manhattan neighborhood of New York City.

(696) Millie is a fan of the pop rock band Imagine Dragons.

(697) The actors playing Karen Wheeler and Eleven's nemesis Angela (the Lenora Hills school bully) both wore the same wig in Stranger Things 4. The wig was just styled differently for each character.

(698) The singer Halsey suggested on a chat show show that Millie could play her in a biopic.

(699) Millie is a fan of the rock band Mumford & Sons.

(700) Although Kali is mentioned briefly in Stranger Things 4 her absence, given all the lab intrigue and focus on Eleven's past, is certainly noticed. If there was ever a time to find room for Kali to make a return to Stranger Things

then season four seemed to be that time.

(701) Confirmation that Millie and Jake Bongiovi were a couple was initially established when they were photographed holding hands while taking a walk in New York.

(702) Millie is a fan of the song Sweater Weather by The Neighbourhood.

(703) It would probably be fair to say that Millie's favourite social media is Instagram.

(704) Whether it was Spain, Dorset, or Florida, Millie was always close to the sea growing up.

(705) Millie said her body clock has conditioned her to go to bed at a reasonable hour because of all of those early starts on television and film productions.

(706) Millie's dad once said he wouldn't let her embark on a music career until she was 16. So far though she has shown no real interest in doing this and probably wouldn't have the time for it anyway.

(707) One of Millie's co-stars in Damsel is Robin Wright. Robin Wright has done many things but will probably always be best known for her role in the cult 1987 film The Princess Bride.

(708) Millie is a fan of Mabes. Mabes is a British female 'folk pop' singer.

(709) Millie is a fan of Duff's Cake Mix. Duff's Cakemix is a do-it-yourself cake decorating studio founded by Food

Network star Duff Goldman.

(710) Millie said that she loves tuna and sweetcorn as a food combination.

(711) Millie said that because the Duffer Brothers are twins and both have beards it is possible to occasionally get them mixed up!

(712) Eleven is capable of remote viewing in Stranger Things. Remote viewing (RV) is the practice of seeking impressions about a distant or unseen subject, purportedly sensing with the mind. Remote viewing is generally regarded to be a pseudoscience in that there is no firm evidence that it is actually real. Remote viewing is also known as telesthesiaand extrasensory perception.

(713) The mall in Stranger Things 3 is similar to the mall in Chopping Mall - a cheesy 1986 horror comedy directed by Jim Wynorski.

(714) In 2018, Millie visited a UNICEF global supply hub in Denmark. While she was there she helped assemble Early Childhood Development kits. "Every day hundreds of life-saving items are sent from this warehouse to children and families around the world, from blankets and clothing, to health and school supplies," said Millie. "To have the opportunity to be a part of this effort with Moncler and UNICEF to offer some sort of relief to those in need, especially a child, is a true privilege. You can't help but think about their circumstances, and what more we can all do to lend a hand."

(715) Millie has been seen wearing a pink sweater with strawberry illustrations.

(716) The Duffer Brothers said that when they were trying to pitch Stranger Things to television networks they had difficulty in explaining the show because it was a show about children but not specifically a show FOR children. Networks obviously had a hard time with this contradiction and couldn't quite seem to grasp the concept.

(717) In season three of Stranger Things, Mike Wheeler begins to worry that Eleven is being pushed beyond her limits. What if the use of her powers was doing damage to her long term health? This is a pop culture nod to Stephen King's Firestarter - where overuse of telepathic powers causes migraine headaches and minute brain haemorrhages.

(718) Vera Farmiga, who played Millie's mother in Godzilla: King of the Monsters, said of Millie - "She's an old pro at it. She's a student. If she wasn't on screen, she was at the screen like looking at the different ratios of film and studying everything. She's a quick study."

(719) Millie said that Mariah Carey has been a useful mentor to her because Mariah also experienced the pressures and demands of fame at a young age.

(720) Millie's Godzilla: King of the Monsters co-star Charles Dance later confessed that he fell asleep at the premiere screening of the film!

(721) Millie was seen wearing a diamond ring early in 2023 - which led to rumours of an engagement. In April 2023, Millie seemed to confirm that she was engaged.

(722) Florence By Mills tends to have a particular focus on eye makeup most of all.

(723) Millie said that a nice garden is an absolute essential for any house she is to live in.

(724) Because she moved around a lot as a kid, Millie doesn't really have a home town. One could probably say that Bournemouth is the closest she has to this.

(725) Millie said she loves a brisk country walk on a frosty winter's day.

(726) Millie's fashion is sometimes described as retro with its 1990s and Y2K influences.

(727) Millie said she had to keep her novel a secret when she was working on it.

(728) It must have been fairly easy for Millie to find a publisher for her novel. Publishers, for very obvious reasons, love celebrity authors.

(729) A magazine who interviewed Millie said she ate a large amount of guacamole while in the makeup chair.

(730) Those who have worked with Millie say she is endlessly chatty and talkative.

(731) Millie is now old enough to vote in elections.

(732) The old Japanese Godzilla movies used stuntmen in monster suits and miniature cities for the special effects. Though a bit silly these films are very charming and endearing from a modern CGI festooned vantage point.

(733) Fancasting sites have suggested that Millie would have made a good Amaya Rose Brimley. Amaya is a Disney

cartoon character.

(734) Millie said she had an almighty 'scream off' with Dacre Montgomery shooting the last scenes between Eleven and Billy in Stranger Things 3. No wonder they both lost their voice!

(735) Sarah Chapman, who features in Enola Holmes 2, was a real person and one of the leaders of the 1888 Bryant & May Matchgirls' strike. Chapman (by then named Sarah Dearman) died in 1945. In 2022 English Heritage announced that the Matchgirls' Strike would be commemorated with a blue plaque at site of the former Bryant and May factory in Bow, London. Sarah Chapman's great-granddaughter was present at the ceremony to unveil the plaque.

(736) Millie said she loves eating pears.

(737) Millie has been photographed wearing a David Bowie t-shirt.

(738) A former British soldier named Matthew Robbens has been head of Millie's security team for a few years. Robbens was previously a bodyguard to Angelina Jolie. Robbens had no idea who Millie was when he was hired because he'd never seen Stranger Things.

(739) Millie has to wear her spectacles when she is driving.

(740) Millie said she loves the old red British public telephone boxes. These red boxes are a vanishing breed now as they were replaced in the 1990s and no one really uses public telephone boxes these days. Red telephone boxes can still be seen though in villages and British

overseas territories.

(741) Millie said she tends to do most of her singing in the car - especially if she is a passenger.

(742) Millie got to cuddle a koala bear when she was in Australia.

(743) It is believed that Millie was paid $3 million to appear in Godzilla vs. Kong.

(744) Millie loves strawberries dipped in chocolate.

(745) When Millie went trick or treating with the Stranger Things kids after the show first came out she was dressed as Princess Leia from Star Wars.

(746) What do the Stranger Things makeup department use to depict the muddy faces of those who endure a trip to the Upside Down? Well, believe it or not, they find that coffee powder is surprisingly effective.

(747) The Duffer Brothers correctly surmised that they would be lynched in they killed Eleven off for good in Stranger Things and made a second season without her so the end of the first season finale includes some crumbs of comfort after her apparent demise. Hopper is seen driving to the forest at night and leaving some Eggo waffles in a provisions box in the snow. The message is clear. Somehow, some way, Eleven is alive. She will return.

(748) Millie was rather mortified when she watched her original Stranger Things audition years later on Beyond Stranger Things. She had very long hair in the audition - all of which was soon to be chopped off!

(749) Hallmark's Keepsake Ornament collection for the 2020 holiday season included a Demogorgon ornament designed for your Christmas tree.

(750) Millie said she often eats a lot of grapes.

(751) It was announced in April 2023 that a Stranger Things cartoon is on the way so we might see an animated version of Millie's character Eleven.

(752) Millie must be one of the few famous British actors who has never done any Shakespeare.

(753) Though it met a somewhat hostile critical reception, Millie said she greatly enjoyed making The Lost Sister episode in Stranger Things 2.

(754) Millie has certainly suffered for her art over the course of Stranger Things when it comes to getting wet. She even had to lay in a water filled pizza dough freezer in Stranger Things 4.

(755) Millie's two most famous roles have both been period pieces.

(756) Millie announced in the Spring of 2023 that she would be doing some 'fan meets' at conventions in Germany, France, Italy, and Japan. She had taken a hiatus from this sort of thing so this was nice news for fans.

(757) Millie said that Eleven's arc in season four of Stranger Things was one that resonated with her because Eleven is coping with growing-up and trying to find her place in the world.

(758) Millie said she always tries to keep a smile on her face and stay positive.

(759) Millie said she doesn't ascribe to method acting. Method acting is a technique in which an actor attempts to fully inhabit the role of the character by becoming that character - even offscreen.

(760) Millie said she did a lot of research on Victorian society in preparation for Enola Holmes.

(761) Millie said it is easier for her to slip back into the character of Eleven than Enola Holmes. She said playing Eleven is second nature but she has to put more thought into playing Enola.

(762) Millie described her Enola Holmes co-star Helena Bonham-Carter as 'bonkers and funny'.

(763) When the pandemic shut down Stranger Things 4, Millie had eight months off work with nothing to do.

(764) Millie said her Stranger Things character Eleven has no fashion sense whatsoever and would probably wear odd socks if left to her own devices!

(765) Millie said that on Stranger Things the Duffer Brothers are always open and generous when it comes to listening to feedback from the actors.

(766) According to Screenrant, Millie turned down a lead role in the proposed film Chronicles of Narnia: The Silver Chair. This film has yet to be made and seems to be stuck in development hell.

(767) Millie said that just before Stranger Things 4 came out, she watched the first three seasons back to back with her younger sister.

(768) Millie said that even if she skips the gym she always gets regular exercise walking her dogs.

(769) One of the reasons why Harry Potter was so successful is that eschews the modern world and technology and gives us heroes who have a simpler (if hardly trouble free) way of life where nature, history, and friendship is more important than what brand of phone you have. The world of Harry Potter, with steam trains, castles, myths and legends, midnight feasts, is timeless and anachronistic. A trip to Hogwarts is like going back in time to escape from the present. This is what gives Harry Potter that comfort blanket feel which charmed readers around the world. A trip to 1980s Hawkins with the characters of Stranger Things also has a cosy comfort blanket feeling for viewers - despite all the monsters and mayhem which inevitably abound.

(770) Stranger Things 4 was much bigger than previous seasons. The scripts amounted to 800 pages.

(771) Millie said it was a great honour to act with David Thewlis in Enola Holmes 2. She said her siblings were especially excited to meet David Thewlis because of his Harry Potter connections.

(772) Millie seems to like a bold orange as a fashion colour.

(773) Millie said that her favourite scene in Stranger Things 2 is when Eleven has a telekinetic temper tantrum during an argument with Hopper at the cabin. She said that David

Harbour actually suggested this scene.

(774) Even when Millie was touring the world promoting the early seasons of Stranger Things she still had to complete her academic homework in her hotel rooms.

(775) Millie said she never set out to be famous. She just wanted to act and fame was an unavoidable byproduct of success as an actor.

(776) The living room in Millie's Atlanta home has arched windows.

(777) Millie said that one of the first things she does when she wakes up is put her contact lenses in.

(778) Millie said she has a habit of impersonating the accents of characters whenever she watches a new TV show.

(779) Millie said that she worked thirteen hour days on Stranger Things 4 and that many scenes were shot over and over to make them perfect.

(780) Millie is by no means unique when it comes to celebrities having a beauty range. Many female actors and singers seem to be beauty entrepreneurs or endorse brands.

(781) In 2016, HELLO! magazine suggested that Millie had a royal lookalike in the form of Spain's Princess Sofia. I can't I saw any resemblance between them myself!

(782) Millie thinks she can do a good impersonation of Noah Schnapp.

(783) Millie said she likes some bohemian qualities in her fashion.

(784) Millie said on Enola Holmes 2 she got so immersed in her producer role that she kept forgetting she had to actually act in the scenes too!

(785) Millie is a fan of the rock band The War on Drugs.

(786) Millie said her favourite costume in the Enola Holmes movies is Enola's red dress.

(787) Millie said that during the production of season one of Stranger Things, Winona Ryder acted as a sort of 1980s Wikipedia for the Duffers and pointed out anachronisms in the script to them. Winona was especially savvy when it came to 1980s household products and music.

(788) Millie thinks her love of spicy food might possibly have something to do with the fact that she was born in Spain.

(789) Millie is not the only famous British actor who went to school in Bournemouth. Christian Bale also went to a school in Bournemouth.

(790) Millie said she isn't the biggest fan of peanuts. She'd rather snack on fruit.

(791) Despite the slavish attention to (period) detail on the show, there are a number of anachronisms in Stranger Things. To give but a few examples, in season one Dustin has a Pez dispenser from 1999 and when Eleven steals waffles from the store you can see brands of modern chewing gum at the cash registers. In season two, Mr Clarke

has a periodic table on his classroom wall containing elements yet to be discovered in 1984. These anachronisms go in both directions when it comes to misplaced eras. The tube of Pringles that Eleven eats in season one are in a container from the late 1960s.

(792) Millie said she tries to ignore 'fashion trolls' who nitpick her outfits.

(793) Harry Bradbeer, the director on the Enola Holmes movies, said you can usually tell by the activity of Millie's eyebrows whether she likes an idea or not!

(794) Millie said that when she first met the Duffer Brothers after being cast in Stranger Things she was surprised at how young they were. The brothers would have been in their early thirties at the time.

(795) Millie said she puts some of her own foibles into the character of Enola Holmes to make her seem human and not perfect.

(796) Millie said that shaving her hair for the first season of Stranger Things wasn't part of her contract or a deal-breaker but more of a creative suggestion which she agreed to.

(797) Millie did a press event in the Philippines in 2016.

(798) Millie said she helped herself to some corduroy jeans and a stripey red and blue T-shirt from one of the stores built for the Starcourt Mall in Stranger Things 3.

(799) Atlanta was nicknamed 'Hollywood East' after Stranger Things and The Walking Dead were produced

there.

(800) When Mike wheeler kisses (rather clumsily on the cheek) Eleven in the first season finale of Stranger Things, the parents of both Millie and Finn Wolfhard were on the set to monitor the scene. Millie and Finn, who both little kids at the time, said this merely made the scene more awkward to shoot!

(801) Millie said she took home one of the corsets as a memento after making the first Enola Holmes film.

(802) Enola Holmes 2 has a 94% critic rating on Rotten Tomatoes. As is often the case though the audience score is a bit more nitpicky at 78%.

(803) The first ever Godzilla film was released way back in 1954.

(804) In Dungeons & Dragons, the Demogorgon has a tail that functions like a whip and can drain the life force out of its foes.

(805) Millie said that secrecy measures to avoid spoilers on Stranger Things 2 became a bit paranoid in the end and everyone became worried there was a 'mole' in the crew leaking information!

(806) Millie said that shooting Kong vs. Godzilla in Hawaii wasn't as exotic as you might think because it was the rainy season and they rarely had a sunny day.

(807) Stacey Solomon attended Millie's 16th birthday party. Stacey Solomon is a singer and television personality.

(808) Millie said that the Stranger Things catering crew make the most amazing salads.

(809) Millie said that she did a lot of pranks on the set of Godzilla: King of the Monsters but the cast and crew pranked her back too. It was generally a fun production.

(810) When it comes to coffee, Millie is fond of an iced caramel latte.

(811) Millie said the cause she is most passionate about is all girls around the world getting an education.

(812) Millie once said in an interview that the worst part of all the travel she does is going through airport security.

(813) Millie said that when Stranger Things became a big thing in 2016 and she was getting recognised all over the place by strangers that getting prescription glasses and her hair growing out mitigated some of this exposure because she soon looked less and less like Eleven in real life.

(814) Millie said that her Stranger Things co-star Gaten Matarazzo is a great singer. Gaten was in a musical on Broadway for a year before he was cast in Stranger Things.

(815) Millie was very excited to meet Hailee Steinfeld at the 2018 Kids' Choice Awards.

(816) Matthew Modine said he has talked to the Stranger Things 'kids' about fame and tried to help them as much as he can. "There's ups and downs in a career," said Modine. "I've had conversations with Millie and the others. And I try to help them to understand they are on a rollercoaster. And the higher you go in your career, the more that drop will

feel really, really frightening."

(817) Brett Gelman, who plays Murray Bauman in Stranger Things, said he learned a lot from working Millie and the young cast cast members and that he found them to be 'impressive' and kind young people.

(818) Millie is a fan of the Disney film Moana.

(819) Millie said you should only go into acting if it is your dream and you shouldn't be pressured into it by parents.

(820) According to IGN, the first Enola Holmes is the 14th most viewed Netflix movie of all time.

(821) Though there were plans for story arcs over a number of seasons, Millie's early TV show Intruders was cancelled after only eight episodes. Television and streaming can be a tough business because if you don't quickly attract and then retain sufficient viewers your show won't last long.

(822) Millie is a fan of the pop band The Vamps.

(823) Millie likes chicken parmigiana. This dish consists of tender breaded chicken covered in marinara with melted mozzarella and Parmesan cheese.

(824) One of the inspirations for Eleven is Madison the Mermaid in the 1984 fantasy film Splash. Like Eleven, Madison struggles to understand the world and uses television to try and expand her vocabulary.

(825) A survey for YouGov America found that 61% of Americans had heard of Millie. You won't be surprised to

hear that Millennials and Gen X accounted for most of the people who knew who she was.

(826) Millie says she isn't very good at whistling.

(827) Millie said that one reason she loves raw carrots is that you lose some of the nutrients if you cook or boil them.

(828) The cast said it actually got quite cold during the Stranger Things 3 shoot but as that season was set in July they had to suffer for their art and wear summer costumes.

(829) Notice how we see Eleven in gunslinger pose in the background as Dustin shouts at the departing and vanquished bullies Troy and James at the quarry in the Stranger Things season one episode The Monster.

(830) There is a Stranger Things parody cookbook called Stranger Fillings.

(831) Millie is a fan of the rock band Arctic Monkeys.

(832) A behind the scenes video on Intruders shows the nine year-old Millie entertaining the crew with an impression of Scary Spice after shooting a scene!

(833) Millie sported a triple braided top-knot hairstyle at the Golden Globes.

(834) Millie said the catering on Godzilla: King of the Monsters was amazing. They had a special pasta bar and also a giant tent which was just for desserts!

(835) Millie said she always gets on very well with the boyfriends and girlfriends of her siblings.

(836) Millie said that one of the most appealing things about being an actor is that it is fun to play someone other than yourself.

(837) Millie said that on the Godzilla movies, although the monster is obviously not there on the set and added in later with digital effects, they do play Godzilla's roars through a loudspeaker to the actors to help get them more into the scene.

(838) In 2019, Millie was seen in Mel's Drive-In diner in West Hollywood with two of Angelina Jolie's children (Zahara and Shiloh). Mel's Drive-In diner is quite famous in Hollywood because it featured in the 1973 George Lucas film American Graffiti.

(839) Millie seems to be fond of wearing baseball caps.

(840) Millie said she still tries to find time to do yoga.

(841) Harry Bradbeer, who directed the Enola Holmes movies, is a veteran television director. His recent work includes Fleabag, Granchester, and Killing Eve. In the 1990s Bradbeer directed some episodes of This Life. This Life was a cult BBC show about young law graduates living together in London and provided an early role for Andrew Lincoln - who later became very famous for playing Rick Grimes in The Walking Dead.

(842) The costume designers on Stranger Things used the 1985 film Just One of the Guys as one of their main reference points for the clothes and fashions of the teenage characters in the show. Just One of the Guys is a teen comedy film directed by Lisa Gottlieb.

(843) A trending phrase in Hollywood now is 'nepo baby'. This refers to nepotism in the film industry in that a large number of actors and directors seem to have famous parents who were also actors or directors - which clearly gave them something of an advantage getting started in the industry. Millie is definitely no 'nepo baby' though as her parents were not famous and she had no relatives in the entertainment industry.

(844) Millie usually seems to take her little sister Ava along to premieres and awards shows.

(845) Millie said that before she created her own beauty range she used to buy her makeup in 'dollar stores'. This obviously means discount stores.

(846) Millie is a fan of the rock band Lord Huron.

(847) The fashion stylist Michelle Kelly has been responsible for choosing some of Millie's outfits.

(848) The first Enola Holmes film used the Severn Valley Railway for the train scenes. The Severn Valley Railway is a standard gauge heritage railway in Shropshire and Worcestershire.

(849) Millie said that when she did her Stranger Things auditions she got four 'callbacks' during the casting process. A callback is very encouraging because it means they want to see you again and like what you've done in the auditions so far.

(850) Millie said she loves a good lemon cake.

(851) Millie wore a red dress at her 16th birthday bash.

(852) Photographs in the media of The Electric State production shooting on a beach showed Millie enjoying a chocolate ice cream cone between scenes.

(853) Millie said that, just like any other teenager, she has had pimples and acne.

(854) Mille had a 'bucking bronco' mechanical bull at her thirteenth birthday party.

(855) Though she has always loved singing Millie said she has never had any singing lessons.

(856) There are still entertainment sites (the BBC have done it a few times too) who occasionally get Millie's name wrong and call her Millie Bobbie Brown rather than Millie Bobby Brown.

(857) The interiors for Ferndell Hall in Enola Holmes were shot at West Horsley Place. West Horsley Place is a Grade I listed building in West Horsley, to the east of Guildford in Surrey.

(858) Henry Cavill's role as Sherlock was expanded in the Enola Holmes sequel. Millie was all for this because she liked the banter between Enola and Sherlock.

(859) Millie seems quite fond of using hair slides.

(860) Millie said she eats an awful lot of lettuce.

(861) Millie is a natural mimic and can't help impersonating people.

(862) Millie's dress for the Stranger Things 3 premiere had

a frilly cape.

(863) During a party for Stranger Things 3, Millie did some dancing with Charlie Heaton. Charlie plays Jonathan Byers in the show.

(864) Millie has been seen enjoying Santa Monica Pier a few times. The Santa Monica Pier is a large double-jointed pier at the foot of Colorado Avenue in Santa Monica, California. It has a funfair and arcades and lots of fun attractions.

(865) Millie was a huge fan of Hannah Montana: The Movie when she was a kid. In a quirk of coincidence, Hannah Montana: The Movie was the first film credit for Millie's Stranger Things co-star Natalia Dyer (who plays Nancy Wheeler).

(866) Matthew Modine said he felt very paternal towards Millie on Stranger Things. He said that in their last scene together the words of Dr Brenner to Eleven echoed his own sentiments towards Millie. In their last scene 'Papa' tells Eleven that he was only trying to protect her and that he is proud of her.

(867) Apart from Winona Ryder and Matthew Modine, most of the cast members of Stranger Things were virtually unknown when they were cast in season one. Even David Harbour wasn't terribly famous - despite a reasonably large body of work. Millie was only really known for Intruders but not many people had seen that show.

(868) When Millie's family moved to Florida, Millie's older sister Paige eventually decided to move back to England alone because she was homesick. Millie said this was a difficult time for the family.

(869) Millie is fond of Rachel Katz Rose Gold Studded earrings.

(870) Millie wore long velvet gloves when she went to the BAFTAS in 2022. This sort of fashion is quite trendy with celebs thanks to shows like The Crown but it's definitely the sort of thing that no one wears in real life. If you get on a bus or go in a pub you are most likely not going to see any women wearing long velvet gloves!

(871) Millie tried some Butterbear when she went to Harry Potter World. At the theme park Butterbeer is a non-alcoholic beverage reminiscent of shortbread and butterscotch.

(872) When Florence By Mills expanded into fashion the promo featuring Millie and some models was shot at a golf course near London by Millie's brother Charlie.

(873) Millie said that, happily, her partial hearing has not really affected or hampered her acting career.

(874) Millie has some pet goats.

(875) Millie was very starstruck when she met the actor Joe Dempsie. Joe Dempsie played Gendry in Game of Thrones.

(876) Millie is a fan of the pop and hip hop duo MKTO.

(877) Millie has been known to wear cropped denim jackets.

(878) Miss Harrison drives a Benz Patent-Motorwagen in Enola Holmes. This was the first production car.

(879) The real location for Basilwether Station in Enola Holmes was Kidderminster Station.

(880) Millie said she quite liked Eggo waffles at first on season one of Stranger Things but soon got sick of them.

(881) On the last day of shooting on season one of Stranger Things, Millie was given a gift by the Duffers of a painting depicting her character Eleven with the boys in the show.

(882) Millie said that when she got her head shaved for season one of Stranger Things going out in the rain felt like getting a shower or head massage.

(883) When Millie turned thirteen she was very excited that Zac Efron was among the celebs wishing her a happy birthday on social media.

(884) Millie said if she hadn't become an actor she would have liked to be a social worker.

(885) Millie said she never fails to be amused by the way her pet rabbit makes a buzzing sound when it is happy.

(886) Millie said one of her first tasks when she wakes up in the morning is to feed her dogs and let them out.

(887) Stranger Things 4 was confirmed only a few months after the release of Stranger Things 3. There was some media speculation that season four would be the last season but this was not the case. The speculation may have originated from comments made by the Duffers back in the early days of the show (in the wake of the huge success of season one) where they conjectured that Stranger Things would probably be a 'four seasons and out' sort of show. As

it transpired though there was still enough story to tell to ensure that we would get a fifth season.

(888) Millie said she cried the first time she watched the trailer for Godzilla: King of the Monsters. It was a great thrill to see herself in a big movie.

(889) During an Instagram Live in 2022, Noah Schnapp was at Millie's house and asked for some toast but Millie didn't have any bread. Noah thought it was a very eccentric for someone not to have any bread in their kitchen!

(890) The character of Godzilla was initially created as a metaphor for atomic weapons.

(891) At her 16th birthday party, Millie's main cake had a row of cupcakes all around it at the bottom.

(892) Millie said because it rained a lot during the production of Kong vs. Godzilla in Hawaii she stayed indoors a lot and baked a cake virtually every day.

(893) The Duffer Brothers said that when they were unsuccessfully and wearily shopping their Stranger Things pitch around Hollywood the most consistent piece of advice they got from studios was to get shot of the kids and just make the show about Jim Hopper. The Duffers stuck to their guns though and insisted that the kids had to stay in the story. The Duffers clearly had the last laugh in this creative disagreement because it was primarily the kids that made Stranger Things such a sensation. People couldn't get enough of those kids in 2016 when the show became a big hit. They were doing TV and radio interviews, conventions, and magazine pieces all over the place. As much as we like Hopper, the show wouldn't have been nearly as much fun if

he was essentially the only main character in the show.

(894) In 2014 it was estimated that the Eggo brand had a 60% share of the frozen waffle market in the United States. This market share would soon increase even further in the years to come thanks to Millie's character Eleven in Stranger Things.

(896) The DemoDogs kill over 40 people in Stranger Things 2. They prove to be no match for Eleven though.

(897) Starburst wrote of Enola Holmes 2 - 'Enola Holmes 2 is great fun. The plot hitches up its skirts and races along from the very first scene and the style and tone very much echo the original with Enola's occasional cheeky fourth wall breaking as she addresses her "audience" and her growing friendship with the timid Lord Tewkesbury (Louis Partridge). Helena Bonham-Carter is back in a slightly larger cameo as Enola's madcap mother Euphoria and David Thewlis' villainous Grail is a baddie in the glorious penny dreadful tradition.

Modern sensibilities are catered for with Adeel Akhtar's all-at-sea Inspector Lestrade, a complete reinvention of Moriarty and, in a mid-credits sequence, the arrival of another Conan Doyle icon not yet introduced into this version of Sherlock's world. But this is really Enola's film and Millie Bobby Brown is a delight; Enola is possessed of the same mercurial intelligence as her brother but her lack of experience leads her to take uncalculated risks and she finds herself in tricky situations more often than she should. It's a lively, atmospheric confection, nicely-realised, and Enola Holmes 2, busier and better structured and paced than the first film, sees this franchise find its feet and opens the door for further adventures to come.'

(898) Millie took home the little pinecone Dash after making Enola Holmes.

(899) Millie said that when she made the show Intruders at the age of nine she stole a prop from the set as a momento!

(900) Millie said that she thought it was a great idea to make the villain Vecna a practical effect (an actor in a suit) rather than a digital special effect because it gave the monster more personality and allowed the actors to have a more authentic interaction with him.

(901) Florence By Mills released a new eye candy eyeshadow stick in April 2023.

(902) Millie said she was rather touched when her younger sister said that Eleven was her favourite character in Stranger Things.

(903) It would probably be fair to say that the California scenes in Stranger Things 4 were in large part completed in more secrecy than the exterior scenes in Atlanta and Jackson. The advantage the producers had for some of the California scenes is that it would have been very difficult to follow the film crew into the desert! The production did an excellent job in keeping the California based cast members under wraps and away from prying eyes. Hardly anything was seen of Millie during the shoot. Pictures of Millie as Eleven are the most highly prized by tabloids and entertainment sites when a season of Stranger Things is shooting so this was no mean feat.

(904) Millie's Atlanta home is painted in 'neutral' shades of beige.

(905) The average length of a Stranger Things episode is 61 minutes. This is mostly due to season four - which had an average episode length of 86 minutes. That was considerably longer than than the previous three seasons. There is no standard length for an episode of the show. They can run for however long the Duffer Brothers decide.

(906) Noah Schnapp described Millie as 'stubborn and clever' in a social media Q&A. Millie wasn't too happy about the 'stubborn' bit!

(907) Millie is a fan of the rock band Grouplove.

(908) Millie said the main thing she looks for in fashion is elegance.

(909) Millie is a fan of the indie band Fitz and the Tantrums.

(910) Stranger Things 4 was the most watched Netflix show in 92 countries.

(911) It is believed that Millie had porcelain veneers to improve her teeth.

(912) The local newspaper in Bournemouth seems to be (rightly) proud of the town's connection to Millie and quite often has articles about her.

(913) Millie said the best thing about theme parks is trying all the food.

(914) Millie is a fan of lemon wedges with her drinks and food.

(915) Vecna's design in Stranger Things 4 owes something

to is DC Comics Swamp Thing. Swamp Thing - a humanoid/plant elemental creature created by writer Len Wein and artist Berni Wrightson - made his first appearance in 1971. The character (who is rather distinctive as he is essentially a human plant!) allowed the various comic arcs he has featured in to touch on genres like horror and themes such as ecology and corporate greed. Alan Moore's work on Swamp Thing in the eighties remains highly acclaimed.

(916) Mariah Carey and her family attended the Enola Holmes 2 premiere in New York.

(917) There are always persistent rumours that Millie is being courted to be in a Star Wars film but so far nothing has come of this.

(918) The first time Millie appeared on a magazine cover was for Interview Magazine way back in 2016.

(919) Millie said going for a drive with Lewis Hamilton was both cool and terrifying.

(920) Millie has quite often posed with a lifesize Eleven Funko figure for publicity shots and premieres.

(921) Millie is a fan of Five Guys. Five Guys is a fast food burger chain.

(922) Pokesdown Community Primary School in Dorset, where Millie went to school, is for 4 to 11 year-olds and has about 400 pupils.

(923) Millie said that in some scenes in Stranger Things season one where Eleven is eating, sometimes she had

nothing at all in her mouth at all and was just pretending to eat.

(924) Millie said that during interviews she has learned to pause before answering a question because this gives her time to think of an answer!

(925) It seems as if, for whatever reason, the media are always looking to anoint a 'Stranger Things Killer' - that is to say a show that is sort of like Stranger Things but better. Why they should seek to do this is not readily obvious. Why do shows have to be compared? Can't we just enjoy them all on their own terms? A show that was often mentioned in connection to Stranger Things in this regard was the moody and interesting German series Dark - which had some vague similarities to Stranger Things but was ultimately a very different beast.

Another show that some people seemed determined to compare to Stranger Things was Paper Girls - an Amazon show based on the brilliant mystery/science fiction comic book series written by Brian K Vaughan and illustrated by Cliff Chiang. Paper Girls starts in 1988 and revolves around four smart and sassy twelve year-old newspaper delivery girls (Erin, MacKenzie, KJ and Tiffany) who live in Stony Stream, Cleveland. One Halloween, while out delivering newspapers on their bikes early in the morning, they are victims of inexplicable events and become catapulted through time, both past and present, where they meet strange creatures, mysterious beings, and (in the biggest horror of all for a young girl) even their older future selves. Paper Girls (the TV show that is) was enjoyable enough but it was no Stranger Things. This was illustrated by the fact that Amazon axed the show after one season because it hadn't captured enough attention.

(926) Millie said being a producer on Enola Holmes felt very natural to her. She loved the artistic control it afforded her.

(927) Millie is a fan of the pop rock band OneRepublic.

(928) Millie said she would like to have a lot of kids one day.

(929) Millie said she likes being tickled.

(930) Millie said she has never once had a falling out or argument with her best friend Noah Schnapp.

(931) Millie has joked that Eleven's name will surely be Jane Wheeler by the end of Stranger Things.

(932) Millie said that a director on Intruders told her to imagine one of her pets being ill to dredge up emotion for a scene. This seems to be an old (and not terribly nice) trick in the world of film production when it comes to child actors.

(933) Millie loves chocolate zeppole. Zeppole are an Italian pastry similar consisting of fried doughnut balls made out of Cream Puff dough.

(934) Millie said that one of the films the Duffer Brothers told her to watch in preparation for Stranger Things was Poltergeist. Poltergeist is a 1982 supernatural horror film directed by Tobe Hooper. Steven Spielberg wrote and produced. The premise of the film? The Freelings are an ordinary family and seem to have a nice life. Or used to anyway. Their young daughter Carol Anne (Heather O'Rourke) starts talking to the TV, a mild earthquake seems

to occur, the TV emits static and strange shapes, things around the house bend and break. And if that wasn't bad enough there's a terrifying tree outside the young son Robie's (Oliver Robins) window. Turns out the house is (gulp) built on an old cemetery and eccentric medium Tangina Barrons (Zelda Rubenstein) might be the family's best hope.

(935) Millie was only supposed to appear in one episode of Once Upon a Time in Wonderland as the young Alice but she was so good they decided to write another episode in which she could feature again.

(936) Millie did a 'geographically friendly' Disney World spot as a very young child actor.

(937) Millie thinks she can do a good impersonation of Winona Ryder.

(938) Millie said she is more of a bath person than a shower person.

(939) Millie said that she doesn't especially enjoy exercise and workouts but it is just something she has to do to stay in shape for her acting.

(940) Millie said that Winona Ryder was always very relatable to the Stranger Things 'kids' because Winona also started acting as a young teenager.

(941) Millie is a fan of the rapper Megan Thee Stallion. Millie was thrilled when she learned that Megan Thee Stallion is a big Stranger Things fan.

(942) It would probably be fair to say that Millie has been

one of the most photographed teenagers in the world over the previous several years. She has done a gazillion photo shoots.

(943) One of Millie's main co-stars in The Electric State is Chris Pratt. Chris Pratt is best known for his role in Marvel's Guardians of the Galaxy movies.

(944) Millie dedicated her Kids Choice Awards to the victims of gun violence.

(945) The incredible appeal of Stranger Things is hard to attribute to any one thing but there are a couple of salient factors which definitely could (in theory) explain why the show has been so amazingly successful. The first factor is obviously that the show is well made and fun. In recent times it has been quite in vogue for mainstream movies and TV shows to be dark or grim and take themselves too seriously. Stranger Things is an antidote to this trend. The show is colourful, funny, and simply out to give you a good time. It isn't trying to preach to the viewer or wallow in misery.

(946) Millie's novel will be published by Harper Collins. Harper Collins are no strangers to celebrity authors because they've published books by Paris Hilton, Justin Beiber, and One Direction amongst many others.

(947) Because of the pandemic hiatus, the Duffer Brothers were able to complete all the Stranger Things 4 scripts prior to production - which is a rarity for a season of the show. As a consequence of this Millie said that the actors knew more than usual about what was going to happen to their characters when production finally resumed again.

(948) Millie said she was a bit apprehensive going into the first Enola Holmes movie because this was the first part she'd played that required her to be funny.

(949) Millie said it was no picnic to squeeze back into a corset again when Enola Holmes 2 began production.

(950) Millie said that to successfully play a character you must completely let go of your own personality.

(951) Millie said a hug is the best way to cheer someone up.

(952) Millie was rather bemused and baffled when she visited a German Comic Con event and found that the audience seemed a little hostile to the Stranger Things character Mike Wheeler for some reason. Millie jokingly said she would tell Finn Wolfhard to avoid Germany!

(953) The vehicle flip by Eleven in the Stranger Things episode The Bathtub is a great moment because it uses the language of action cinema against an offbeat backdrop. It is a stunt, or 'trailer moment', straight out of a summer blockbuster film. How many times have we seen a large vehicle flip over in an action film? It's hardly new. What makes this stunt special and so rewarding is the context. These aren't Transformers fighting in a green screen big city CGI overload. The Batmobile isn't racing through Gotham. John McClane isn't involved in a freeway demolition derby. These are little kids on bikes in suburbia!

(954) Millie was photographed enjoying some vanilla ice cream on her first visit to Japan.

(955) Millie said that when she's in England she likes a good ramble in the woods.

(956) Millie was once photographed reading Stephen King's IT on a plane. Finn Wolfhard was in the film version of this book.

(957) Millie has posted social media videos of her watching England play big international football matches. She certainly gets into the spirit of things by wearing an England shirt and singing the national anthem.

(958) Millie likes colourful vases in her home.

(959) Millie said she loves mangos.

(960) The Duffer Brothers said that Millie and Finn Wolfhard were like little film students on Stranger Things and always soaking up a lot of technical knowledge. This will serve them well in future years if they move behind the camera.

(961) Millie said that she has done some singing in the studio with Mariah Carey - purely for fun.

(962) Millie jokingly said of having Godzilla as a co-star - "He's a bit of a diva. Hard to work with occasionally, but all right."

(963) When Millie visited the Stranger Things Experience in New York City in 2022 she wore a jumpsuit with a floral theme.

(964) Millie said that her late grandmother Ruth told her stories about what it was like to grow up during the war.

(965) Millie said she loves having a big wedge of tomato in her sandwiches.

(966) Millie is a fan of the Canadian singer Ruth B.

(967) Although the fifth season of Stranger Things will be the last it doesn't seem implausible at all to think that Millie will play the character again one day in a reunion.

(968) Millie is a fan of the song Riptide by Vance Joy.

(969) Millie is rather unusual for a high profile British actor in that she didn't go to drama school.

(970) After she finished shooting the first season of Stranger Things, Millie went back to singing songs on her old YouTube channel. It was only when Stranger Things dropped on Netflix and she became famous virtually overnight that this YouTube channel was quietly abandoned.

(971) Millie's boyfriend Jake Bongiovi drew praise in 2018 when he arranged a walkout at his school in a protest over gun violence.

(972) Millie went to the Stranger Things 4 premiere with Jake Bongiovi.

(973) Millie said it was a bit weird to do the teenage kissing scenes with Finn Wolfhard in Stranger Things 3 because she'd known him since she was ten and they are good platonic friends.

(974) Millie said that on Stranger Things working with the Duffer Brothers, one of the brothers is a soft-touch and the other is little bit stricter. She was too diplomatic to say which was which though!

(975) Millie said that Henry Cavill is like an older brother to her in real life too.

(976) Millie has been known to wear a black pageboy cap.

(977) Stranger Things 4 actually bucks a trend on IMDB because in all the previous three seasons the finale was always the highest rated episode on the site. That isn't the case with season four - where the finale The Piggyback only ranks third after The Massacre at Hawkins Lab and Dear Billy.

(978) Notice how Steve Harrington looks slightly baffled when Eleven returns at the end of the Stranger Things 2 episode The Mind Flayer. This is because Steve has never met Eleven before.

(979) Millie was apparently the most web searched actress in the world at one point after Stranger Things came out and was a big overnight phenomenon.

(980) One of the many monster influences on the Demogorgon in Stranger Things was the Pale Man (aka Eyeball Hands) in Pan's Labrynth.

(981) Millie has joked that she would like to be in Birdy 2 with Matthew Modine. Birdy is a cultish 1980s drama film that Modine was in.

(982) A season of Stranger Things is designed to play like one long movie - which makes it perfect to binge. The episodes often end with cliffhangers which make you want to watch the NEXT episode straight away. The Duffer Brothers say they are unashamed bingers themselves and don't watch television in the old fashioned way (that is one

episode a week) anymore. Technology has definitely changed the way we consume entertainment. We like having the ability to watch as many episodes of something as we want and Stranger Things (which is released on a streaming platform in one block - or two when it comes to season four) taps into this trend.

(983) Millie seems to be a fan of Roger Vivier fashion and accessories.

(984) Millie seems to be quite fond of leather jackets.

(985) Millie wore a cowboy style hat at her nineteenth birthday bash.

(986) Millie said that during the production of Stranger Things 4 she would often go food shopping with Matthew Modine. She said people in the grocery store did a double take when they saw Papa and Eleven browsing cereal in the aisles!

(987) Variety wrote of Godzilla vs. Kong - 'Just because Warner Bros. is treating the adversaries as bona fide A-listers doesn't mean the rock-'em-sock-'em extravaganza amounts to anything more than a dumb-fun B-movie. Nor should it. Considering the havoc a microscopic virus has wreaked on the past year, being caught between two 400-foot titans doesn't seem so bad.'

(988) The Old Royal Naval College in Greenwich was one of the locations for the first Enola Holmes film.

(989) Stranger Things co-creator Matt Duffer said that when you audition children for acting roles you can tell in seconds if they are any good or not.

(990) The young cast members in Stranger Things often
Facetime one another sometimes because they all live so far
away. Gaten is in New Jersey, Finn usually in Canada, and
Millie often in England or Georgia.

(991) One of the Netflix sound stages caught fire during the
production of Stranger Things 4. Thankfully, no one was
injured.

(992) When Intruders first aired on television, a poster on
Reddit wrote - 'The little girl though (Millie Brown) -
seriously blowing my mind with her acting. So good.'

(993) Millie owns a Houndstooth Wool-Blend Blazer.

(994) Millie said she kept her Enola Holmes ambitions
secret for about three years until she secured the rights.

(995) In the brilliant book 'Upside Down: The Unofficial and
Unauthorised Stranger Things Companion' by James
Forster, the author wrote - 'Nothing quite screams Stranger
Things like the sight of Millie Bobby Brown floating in a
sensory deprivation water chamber!'

(996) Millie wore a Valentino Fall 2019 tulle gown for The
Chinese premiere of Godzilla: King of the Monsters.

(997) Millie seems to be quite fond of platform shoes for
chat shows.

(998) Millie wore a pink Louis Vuitton dress to the Enola
Holmes 2 New York premiere.

(999) Millie said that when her parents heard about the
casting for a show called Montauk (obviously later to be

called Stranger Things) she wasn't very keen to do an audition and was tired of acting and rejections but her parents told her if she did this one last audition she could then go out and play and do whatever she wanted. Millie therefore relented and agreed to do a cam audition. Millie deciding to do that audition was what you call a true 'sliding doors' moment because it led to her becoming a world famous millionaire and highly successful much in demand young actor. Who knows what might have happened if Millie hadn't done the Montauk audition? She might have drifted out of acting altogether and done something completely different with her life.

(1000) Whether or not Millie's career will have longevity remains to be seen but she clearly has the talent and work ethic to be successful for decades to come.

Photo Credit

https://commons.wikimedia.org/wiki/File:Millie_Bobby_Br
own_Pandora_2020_27s.jpg

2 July 2020

TheOfficialPandora